Dublin City Guide, Ireland

Tourism

Author
Ethan Brown.

Publisher:
SONIT
2162 Davenport House, 261 Bolton Road. Bury. Lancashire. BL8 2NZ. United Kingdom.

Table of Content

Summary

Travel is more than the seeing of sights, it is a change that goes on, deep and permanent in the idea of living.
The ability to move around from one place to the other is the biggest virtue one can ever have. All humans and animals have been blessed with this ability, but humans are always a step forward. We humans, possess an extraordinary virtue of seeing, experiencing and learning from it, and this is precisely what makes our journeys more satisfying and enriching.

Humans have been traveling from time immemorial for a variety of reasons. In an age when there was no infrastructure and no means of transport, even for long-distance journeys, people used to travel on foot or on animal backs. Sometimes, these journeys were extremely long and tiring and it took a person, weeks or even months together to reach the destination. A person who went on a long-distance journey returned home after years. Till then, his family had either no or very little knowledge regarding his whereabouts and well-being. In some extreme cases, a person would never return. In spite of all these barriers and difficulties, people traveled; not always because they needed to, but many times, also because they loved to. And why not? Traveling not only takes us to distant lands and acquaints us with different people, but it also tends to break the monotony of our lives

Introduction

Dublin, Irish Dubh Linn, Norse Dyfflin ("Black Pool"), also called Baile Átha Cliath ("Town of the Ford of the Hurdle"), city, capital of Ireland, located on the east coast in the province of Leinster. Situated at the head of Dublin Bay of the Irish Sea, Dublin is the country's chief port, centre of financial and commercial power, and seat of culture. It is also a city of contrasts, maintaining an uneasy relationship between reminders of earlier political and economic conditions and symbols of present-day life and prosperity. Area city, 45.5 square miles (118 square km). Pop. (2006) 506,211; Greater Dublin, 1,187,126; (2011) 527,612; Greater Dublin, 1,273,069.

Character of The City

Dublin is a warm and welcoming city, known for the friendliness of its people and famous for its craic ("crack") that mixture of repartee, humour, intelligence, and acerbic and deflating insight that has attracted writers, intellectuals, and visitors for centuries. It has faded grandeur and a comfortably worn sense. Some one-fourth of the residents of the Republic of Ireland live in the Greater Dublin urban area, providing a good deal of bustle. The city's heart is divided north-south by the River Liffey, with O'Connell's Bridge connecting the two parts. Pubs (where much of the city's social life is conducted), cafés, and restaurants abound, and Irish musicality rarely allows silence.

On the north side, near the General Post Office, stand most of the remaining Georgian houses, built in the 18th century around squares, now side by side with glass and concrete offices and apartment blocks. Some of the finest monumental buildings stand on the north riverbank, as do the city's poorest parts, maintaining a curious juxtaposition between the echoes of the politics and economic life of the past aristocratic and impoverished and the manifestations of the prosperous city of the present.

Ireland's national theatre, the Abbey, is just east of O'Connell Street, marked since 2002 by the Spire of Dublin, a 394-foot (120-metre) stainless steel landmark that proclaimed the street's transformation with a pedestrian plaza and tree-lined boulevard. Together with a rash of new high-rise buildings, the spire has changed the character of the city and of the north side. Though Dublin has undergone modernization, and some areas such as the narrow and winding streets of the Temple Bar district west of Trinity College regularly play host to rowdy and raucous crowds, a strong sense of history and of a centuries-old capital pervades.

Landscape

City site

Dublin's geographic site is superb. Situated at the head of a beautiful bay, the city straddles the River Liffey where it breaks eastward through a hill-ringed plain to the shores of the Irish Sea. (The dark bog water draining into the river made the "black pool" that gave the city its name.) Almost certainly, this opening from the sea leading through the mountains to the fruitful central plains of Ireland originally attracted Viking raiders and Norse settlement. Each year the suburbs jut farther into the countryside, but to the south there is a natural limit posed by the Dublin and Wicklow mountains, which ring the city and provide some of its most beautiful vistas.

Climate

Dublin enjoys a maritime temperate climate. The average temperature is lowest in January February, 42 °F (6 °C), and highest in July August, peaking at about 68 °F (20 °C). Most sunshine is in May and June and averages four hours a day. The mean annual rainfall is 30 40 inches (760 1,000 mm), although more falls in the surrounding mountains. There are fewer than 10 days of snow per year.

City layout

Apart from the port area and the docks, Dublin is a low-built, steepled city, with few buildings dating from before the 17th century. The

Roman Catholic churches are 19th- and 20th-century structures. The 17-story Liberty Hall (built 1961 65 as a trade-union headquarters), long Dublin's tallest building, has been joined by a spate of new high-rise offices and apartments. Still, most of the buildings are no higher than 5 or 6 stories.

The three elements that constitute the architectural legacy of Dublin Norse, Norman, and Georgian all meet in Dublin Castle. In the first two decades of the 13th century, the Normans obliterated the Norse stronghold and raised a château-fort. When the Georgians built the present red-brick castle, they left two towers of the old structure standing. The castle the seat of British authority in Ireland until 1922 is now used for ceremonial occasions, especially the inauguration of the republic's presidents, who reside at Áras an Uachtaráin ("the President's House," formerly the Viceregal Lodge) in Phoenix Park, and for local and international conferences. The castle also is the home of a number of cultural organizations, notably the Chester Beatty Library.

Close to the castle a Norse king of Dublin built Christ Church Cathedral (c. 1030), which was replaced about 140 years later by a more magnificent Norman structure. By the 19th century the edifice was in ramshackle condition; it was restored in the 1870s at enormous cost. Its neighbour, St. Patrick's, erected just outside the city walls, was also originally a Norse church that may have been built on an earlier Celtic foundation. Rebuilt by the Normans in 1191, it was enlarged and partially rebuilt over the centuries. It was in a state of collapse when Sir Benjamin Lee Guinness, the brewing magnate and a lord mayor of Dublin, financed its restoration in the mid-19th century. Christ Church is the cathedral for the diocese of Dublin and Glendalough, whereas St. Patrick's, unusually, is not the seat of a bishop.

Both have been Church of Ireland (Anglican) churches since the Reformation. In 1949 the funeral of Douglas Hyde, the first president of the Republic of Ireland, was held at St. Patrick's. Because of the Roman Catholic Church's prohibition of its members' attending Protestant services, the whole Irish government, apart from its two Anglican members, attended in the foyer of the cathedral. The Pro (for Provisional) Cathedral on Marlborough Street, to the east of O'Connell Street on the north side, is the principal Roman Catholic church. It was completed in 1825 and is the seat of the archbishop of Dublin and primate of Ireland.

The area between St. Patrick's and the Guinness Brewery on the Liffey is known as the Liberties, located outside the old city walls and so named because it was subject to private jurisdiction and not to the king or the town. In the years after World War II, large tracts of this district were cleared for low-cost housing.

Dublin's early private speculators had a sense of order and beauty as acute as their sense of profit. The city's streets were broad and its garden squares spacious. For their time (the 18th century), the houses were ultramodern elegant yet simple Georgian and Neoclassical structures designed in the manner of the great English architects Inigo Jones and Sir Christopher Wren. The sweeps of red-brick houses, ranged in squares and long terraces and built with well-proportioned windows, made a harmonious whole that still stands as a happy achievement of urban architecture.

In the southern half of the town, between Trinity College and St. Stephen's Green, Joshua Dawson, one of Dublin's leading citizens, built an impressive house that was completed in 1710. The city soon bought the house to serve as residence of the lord mayor, and, as the Mansion House, it still does. The first Irish republican parliament, the Dáil Éireann, met there in 1919.

Dawson's neighbours, the equally prominent Molesworths, followed his example and began building houses and entire streets. In 1745 48 the earl of Kildare erected a palace at the end of Molesworth Street; Kildare House, renamed Leinster House when the earl became the duke of Leinster, is thought to have been the model for the White House in Washington, D.C. It is now the seat of the republic's parliament (Oireachtas). Twin Victorian buildings, which were constructed on either side of Leinster House in the 1880s, contain the National Library and the National Museum of Ireland. Merrion, immediately to the east, and Fitzwilliam, to the south, are two of the great 18th-century squares.

The oldest and largest of the city's squares is St. Stephen's Green, recorded in 1224 as common grazing land but enclosed and bordered with houses in the 1660s. Most of the imposing mansions now surrounding it were built in the 18th century. By 1887 the parkland was run down, and the Guinness family, whose former residence on the south side now houses the Department of Foreign Affairs, paid for its rehabilitation.

The city's north-south axis runs from the western side of St. Stephen's Green down Grafton Street and through College Green to the Liffey, across O'Connell Bridge to the river's northern bank, and then along O'Connell Street to Parnell Square. Grafton Street, long Dublin's premier shopping district, was made pedestrian-only in the 1990s, and it has become a lively thoroughfare hosting street entertainers. It emerges onto College Green between the University of Dublin (Trinity College) and the 1729 Parliament House, which is now the privately run Bank of Ireland's headquarters.

Along the Liffey's northern quays stand James Gandon's Neoclassical masterpieces of the Custom House (1781 91) and the Four Courts (1786 1802). The Custom House was burned out in 1921 by republicans who wished to destroy administrative records; the Four Courts was ruined by shellfire and mines at the outbreak of civil war in June 1922. Both have since been rebuilt.

O'Connell Street first called Drogheda and then Sackville Street is a stretch of shops, cinemas, and snack bars. The only building of any distinction to survive the warfare that swept the street in 1916 and again in 1922 was the General Post Office, seized as headquarters of the 1916 rebellion. Badly damaged, it was reconstructed behind its surviving 1815 classical facade in 1929. Opposite the post office stood Nelson's Pillar, a landmark for generations of Dubliners. Built in 1808, it was mysteriously blown up late one night in 1966. At the beginning of the 21st century, Dublin Corporation (now Dublin City Council) began upgrading both the street and its shops, cutting down the century-old London plane trees that lined the centre and erecting the Spire.

At the top of O'Connell Street, Bartholomew Mosse constructed his Rotunda Hospital, the "Lying-In," which remains a maternity hospital to this day. The rotunda itself is now the historic Gate Theatre. Behind the hospital is Parnell (formerly Rutland) Square, laid out in 1750, with many of its original Georgian houses still intact. One of these, built for the earl of Charlemont in 1762 65, now houses the Municipal Gallery of Modern Art.

The 18th-century city commissioners circumscribed the growing city with the North and South Circular roads. Synge Street, close to the South Circular Road, was the birthplace of the dramatist George Bernard Shaw. The Grand Canal was constructed to the south and the

Royal Canal to the north of these peripheral roads; both canals enter the Liffey at the harbour entrance and both connect with the River Shannon. Only the Grand is now navigable.

Dublin's Phoenix Park is Europe's largest enclosed urban park. It is roughly ovoid in shape, with a land perimeter of 7 miles (11 km), and is situated on the north bank of the Liffey, about 2 miles (3 km) west of the city centre. In September 1979, during the first visit by a reigning pontiff to Ireland, the religious service conducted by Pope John Paul II in the park attracted an estimated 1.25 million people, the largest gathering ever recorded in the country.

Duels took place in the park, and in 1882 it was the scene of an assassination that involved the stabbing of the British chief secretary of Ireland, Lord Frederick Cavendish, and his undersecretary, T.H. Burke (see Phoenix Park murders). Initially a royal deer park, Phoenix Park was opened to the public in 1747. Its zoo, celebrated for lion breeding, opened in 1831 and effectively doubled its size in 2001 when the African Plains section opened on land donated by the president of Ireland from the presidency's official holdings. The 205-foot (62-metre) Wellington Monument is at the southeast end of the park, commemorating Arthur Wellesley, 1st duke of Wellington. Nearby is Islandbridge, the site of World War I memorial gardens designed by Sir Edwin Luytens.

People

Demography

During the second half of the 20th century, the population of Dublin and the surrounding area grew annually by about 1 percent, the same rate as the country generally. Initially the trend in migration was from the countryside to the city. During the last quarter of the 20th century, however, central city areas began to lose population, while new suburbs southwest and north of Dublin grew. Urban regeneration at the end of the 20th century attracted new dwellers to the inner city.

Religion

The administrative bodies of Ireland's main religious groups are based in Dublin. The city, in common with the rest of the country, is overwhelmingly Roman Catholic, though Dublin remains the most religiously diverse part of Ireland. The non-Catholic population steadily declined after 1922, but censuses in the early 21st century showed a marked increase in the number of Protestants and Muslims living in the city. Evangelical and charismatic Christian groups began growing in the 1970s, and together with immigration this has increased diversity. The number of Dubliners professing no religion, especially among the young, has also increased.

Economy

Manufacturing

Dublin's major traditional industries brewing (the Guinness Brewery has operated at St. James's Gate since 1759), distilling, food processing, and textile manufacturing have all declined since the 1970s, resulting in inner-city blight. The recession of the 1980s brought a slump in the building trades. Several industrial estates, however, were built in the suburbs around the city and, with the help of government grants and general economic improvement in the 1990s, attracted new enterprises, notably information technology, electronics, chemicals, engineering, and financial services firms.

Finance and other services

Dublin is the headquarters for Ireland's chief financial and commercial institutions. The economic pace has quickened markedly since 1973, when the country joined the European Economic Community (EEC; later succeeded by the European Union [EU]). In addition to the major clearing banks, all of which have their main offices in Dublin, there has been a rapid increase in the number of other banks, principally from EU countries. The Irish Stock Exchange, an integral part of the British Stock Exchange system, is also located in central Dublin and is one of the oldest such markets in the world, trading continuously since 1793.

Traffic through the port of Dublin has grown steadily since the 1990s. In 1987 the International Financial Services Centre was established in the former northern dock area, under the Custom House Development Authority. This venture reflected the country's commitment to the single European market, with its attendant abolition of duties and tariffs within the EU. It began the regeneration of the docks as a flourishing business and residential area. Millions of tourists flock to Dublin annually, and the city has responded with new hotels, events, activities, and transport systems.

Transportation

The city council has prime responsibility for traffic management in Dublin. Major roads are a national responsibility, but this inevitably has a great effect on the capital. The Dublin Port Tunnel, Ireland's largest civil engineering project, opened in 2006 and links the port to the national motorway network. The Dublin Area Rapid Transit (DART) train service runs along the coast from Malahide and Howth in County Fingal to Greystones, County Wicklow, in the south. A tram system from St. Stephen's Green in the centre of the city began operating in

2004. Connolly and Heuston are the capital's two railway stations; Connolly serves the north and northwest, Heuston the south, southwest, and west. Irish Railways (Iarnród Éireann), a subsidiary of Córas Iompair Éireann (CIE), the national transport company, provides suburban services and intercity connections with the rest of the country and Northern Ireland. City bus services provide extensive service. Dublin's international airport is just north of the city at Collinstown.

Administration and Society

National and local government

Dublin is the headquarters for government departments, their advisory committees, and associated agencies. The two houses of the Irish parliament, the Dáil and the Seanad (Senate), meet at Leinster House. The judiciary is based at the Four Courts. More than 40 countries maintain embassies, and several others are represented by consuls, both honorary and professional.

The Dáil abolished the county of Dublin in 1994, substituting the Dublin Region of three new counties Dún Laoghaire Rathdown, Fingal, and South Dublin and the City of Dublin, which has both county and city government powers. The Dáil also replaced city corporations with city councils as the administrative bodies in 2002. The Dublin Regional Authority coordinates the plans, reviews the budgets, and monitors the spending of EU funds by the three counties and Dublin City Council (formerly Dublin Corporation). The council is the largest local authority in Ireland, consisting of more than 50 councillors elected every five years by proportional representation. The council is led by a lord mayor chosen annually by the councillors from among themselves. The lord mayor chairs meetings, but the role is otherwise principally ceremonial; a city manager performs the executive functions. Through the Local Appointments Commission, the state's Department of the Environment names the managers. Just under one-third of the Irish electorate lives in the Dublin Region's 12 constituencies, which are represented by 47 members of the proportionally elected Dáil.

Municipal services

Police services are a national responsibility, and Ireland is divided into six police regions. The Dublin Metropolitan Region embraces the city, the whole of the Dublin Region, and small portions of County Kildare to the west and County Wicklow to the south.

The city is home to numerous parks. St. Stephen's Green, first enclosed in the 1660s and laid out in 1880 in its present form with flower beds, trees, a lake, a fountain, a bandstand dating from 1887, and memorials to various Dubliners, is in the centre of the city. Immediately to the south are the Iveagh Gardens, perhaps the least known of Dublin's parks. Landscaped in 1863, they include a maze, archery grounds, woodland, fountains, a grotto, and a cascade. The National Botanic Gardens in Glasnevin to the north of the city contain some 20,000 different plants.

The Dublin Fire Brigade is run by the city council on behalf of the three other local authorities in the urban area. The brigade also provides an emergency ambulance service for the Greater Dublin area, and several fire stations have ambulances that operate.

Health

In 2005 the Health Boards system responsible for providing national health care was abolished. In its place a Health Service Executive (HSE) was established. Dublin is divided into two HSE regions. The regions have their own public health ambulance service. There are several private ambulance services, including air ambulances. Dublin contains numerous public and private hospitals, including four university hospitals the Mater Misericordiae, Beaumont, St. Vincent's, and St. James's. All have departments of international repute ranging from children's care to transplants and diagnostics. The Mater is associated with University College Dublin and is the national centre for cardiothoracic surgery. Dublin's Royal College of Surgeons is one of the five recognized colleges of the National University of Ireland.

Beaumont Hospital, opened in 1987, is the principal undergraduate and postgraduate teaching and research centre associated with the Royal College, whose campus it shares. It is the national centre for neurosurgery. St. Vincent's is the teaching hospital of University College Dublin and a leading biomedical research institute. St. James's

Hospital, which replaced several older hospitals, is associated with Trinity College and houses the Centre for Advanced Clinical Therapeutics, the Dementia Services Information and Development Centre, the National Centre for Pharmacoeconomics, and the National Medicines Information Centre. St. Patrick's Hospital, founded in 1746 by a bequest from Jonathan Swift, is a private psychiatric centre still functioning on its original site, just south of Heuston Station.

Education

Founded in 1592, Trinity College is Ireland's oldest university, though most of its distinguished buildings date from the 18th century. It possesses the largest collection of publications in Ireland, including the early 9th-century Book of Kells and the mid-12th-century Book of Leinster, both lavishly illustrated religious manuscripts. For centuries Trinity was regarded as a bastion of the "Protestant Ascendancy" that governed and effectively owned and controlled most of Ireland. In fact, the college was among the most liberal in the British Isles. In the 18th century, while Roman Catholics were barred by law from taking degrees, they could still attend the college. The Catholic Relief Act (1793) enabled Catholics to take degrees but not to have full standing. All such religious exclusions were dropped in 1873. Nevertheless, Trinity remained almost exclusively Protestant until the Roman Catholic Church's ban on attending was lifted in 1970.

University College Dublin, established as the Catholic University of Ireland in the 1850s and now a constituent college of the National University of Ireland, is the largest campus in Ireland, with more than 20,000 students. In 1940 Eamon de Valera founded the Institute for Advanced Studies with Austrian physicist Erwin Schrödinger (who became an Irish citizen) as the director of its School for Theoretical Physics. In 1989 the capital's newest university, Dublin City University, was created from the National Institute for Higher Education. Also in the city are a number of other institutions of higher education, including colleges of technology, teacher-training colleges, and specialized vocational colleges.

Cultural Life

Dublin played a leading role in the cultural renaissance that began in 1884 with the establishment of the Gaelic Athletic Association (Cumann Lúthchleas Gael) for the revival of historically Irish games. It was broadened in 1893 with the foundation of the Gaelic League (Conradh na Gaeilge), which promotes the Irish language and Irish folklore. The National Gallery, the Irish Museum of Modern Art, the Project Arts and City Arts centres, and many privately owned galleries reflect the liveliness of the visual arts in Dublin. Temple Bar has been developed with a mix of boutiques, galleries, and studios.

Literature, theatre, and music

At the centre of Ireland's rich Anglo-Irish literary, philosophical, and political history, Greater Dublin was the birthplace of three winners of the Nobel Prize for Literature: playwrights Samuel Beckett and George Bernard Shaw and poet William Butler Yeats. Other notable figures associated with the city include the satirists Jonathan Swift and Brendan Behan, the poet and dramatist Oscar Wilde, the playwright Sean O'Casey, the political theorist Edmund Burke, and the novelist

James Joyce, author of the renowned short-story collection Dubliners (1914) and of the groundbreaking novel Ulysses (1922), which presents a day in the life of Dublin in 1904 through three characters whose stories parallel events in Homer's Odyssey. More recently, Dublin has provided the setting for the fiction of Maeve Binchy and Roddy Doyle.

Early in the 20th century, the cultural renaissance in Dublin continued with the opening of the famous Abbey Theatre, an enterprise associated particularly with the playwrights John Millington Synge and Augusta, Lady Gregory. In addition to producing their works, the Abbey later staged the first performances of major plays. The old theatre burned down in the early 1950s, but with government help a new theatre was opened in 1966; it houses both the main Abbey stage and the smaller, experimental Peacock Theatre. In 1928 Micheál MacLiammóir and Hilton Edwards started the renowned Gate Theatre Company, which continues to flourish. Orson Welles and James Mason began their acting careers there. The state-sponsored Arts Council, with headquarters in Dublin, subsidizes the Abbey, the Gate, and a number of small theatrical groups in the region.

Among the city's main commercial theatres are the Gaiety, which stages annual opera seasons, and the Olympia. In 1980 the National Concert Hall was opened, finally giving the capital, after decades of unsuccessful attempts, a major concert venue. Radio Telefís Éireann, the national radio and television station, is also based in Dublin. It employs the country's principal symphony orchestra. The city also has produced a number of internationally famous folk and pop musicians, including Finbar Furey, Sinéad O'Connor, the Boomtown Rats, and U2.

Publishing

The country's principal book publishers, periodicals, and newspapers, including several evening, national daily, and Sunday papers, are based in Dublin. A number of small but influential literary and current affairs magazines are published, both in Irish and in English. Since the 1970s there has been an increase in the number of publishing houses devoted to literature, especially poetry.

Sports

Phoenix Park holds annual motor races. Horse racing flourishes at Leopardstown in South Dublin, about 6 miles (10 km) from the city centre, and at Fairyhouse, about 15 miles (24 km) from the city centre in County Meath. There is also a greyhound track at Harold's Cross. The traditional Gaelic games of hurling and Gaelic football are played at Croke Park, on the north bank of the Royal Canal. International rugby and football (soccer) matches are held at Lansdowne Road, and Belfield at University College Dublin attracts major competitions. Golf is popular.

History

Dublin was founded by the Vikings. They founded a new town on the south bank of the Liffey in 841. It was called Dubh Linn, which means black pool. The new town of Dublin was fortified with a ditch and an earth rampart with a wooden palisade on top. In the late 11th stone walls were built around Dublin. The Danes also erected an artificial hill where the men of Dublin met to make laws and discuss policy.

In Viking Dublin living conditions were primitive. The houses were wooden huts with thatched roofs. None of them had chimneys or glass windows. In Dublin there were craftsmen like blacksmiths and carpenters, jewelers and leather workers. Other craftsmen made things like combs from bone or deer antler. There was also a wool weaving industry. In Dublin there was also a slave trade.

The Danes were slowly converted to Christianity and the first Bishop of Dublin was appointed in 1028. In his time the first Christchurch Cathedral was built. In the wars between Irishmen and Vikings the little town of Dublin was sacked several times. Yet each time it recovered. Dublin soon grew to be the largest and most important town in Ireland. It may have had a population of 4,000 in the 11th century. That seems very small to us but it was a large town by the standards of the time when settlements were very small. By the late 11th century there was a suburb of Dublin north of the Liffey. In those days the people of Dublin traded with the English towns of Chester and Bristol.

Dublin in The Middle Ages

In 1166, MacMurrough, King of Leinster was forced to leave his kingdom and flee abroad, In 1169 he enlisted the help of a Norman, The Earl of Pembroke, known as Strongbow, and they invaded Ireland. When the Norman army approached Dublin the Archbishop was sent out to negotiate. But while the leaders talked some Norman soldiers took matters into their own hands and broke through the defenses into the town. They set about killing the townspeople. The Viking king and his followers fled by sea.

In 1171 Mac Murrough died and Strongbow declared himself king of Leinster. The Viking king returned to Ireland with an army and attempted to recapture Dublin. The Norman army went out to meet them. The Vikings were crushed and their king was captured and executed. The native Irish under their High king O'Connor laid siege to Dublin but the Normans sallied out and routed them. The English king was afraid that Strongbow would become too powerful and might call himself king of Ireland. To prevent that happening the English king came over to Ireland himself. Most of the Irish rulers submitted to him and he became Lord of Ireland. The English king gave Dublin to the merchants of Bristol. It became their colony. Afterwards many people from Bristol and Southwest England came to live in Dublin. For centuries afterwards Dublin was ruled by the English or those of English descent. The Viking inhabitants were afraid of the new English rulers and they moved to the north side of the Liffey. This new suburb became known as Ostmantown (Ostman is an old word for Viking). In time this became corrupted to Oxmantown.

In 1152 the Bishop of Dublin was made an Archbishop. Between 1172 and 1191 the Cathedral of Christchurch was rebuilt. In 1213 the parish Church of St Patrick was also made a cathedral.

In 1190 Dublin was devastated by fire (always a hazard when most buildings were made of wood). However Dublin was soon rebuilt. The Normans built a wooden fortress in Dublin. In the early 13th century it was rebuilt in stone. The English king also rebuilt the walls of Dublin and strengthened them. Furthermore in 1229 Dublin gained its first mayor. Dublin grew rapidly and may have had a population of 8,000 by the 13th century.

Wine from France into was imported into Dublin. Iron was also imported, as was pottery. Exports included hides, grain and pulses. There were weekly markets in Dublin and after 1204 a fair. In the

Middle Ages fairs were like a market but they were held only once a year for a few days and people would come from all over the country to buy and sell there.

In 1224 a conduit was built to bring fresh water into Dublin. In the 14th century the main streets were paved. But like all medieval towns Dublin was very unsanitary. Every householder was supposed to clean the street in front of their house although it is doubtful if many did! From time to time people were fined for leaving nuisances such as piles of dung outside their houses. In 1305 the town appointed 3 watchmen to patrol the streets at night, although it is doubtful if they were very effective.

In 1317 Dublin was besieged by a Scottish army. Following their victory at Bannockburn in 1314 the Scots invaded Ireland. Desperate efforts were made to repair the walls around Dublin and the bridge over the Liffey was destroyed to prevent the Scots using it. Finally the authorities set fire to the suburbs of Dublin (in case they provided cover for an advancing army). Unfortunately the fire got out of hand and destroyed far more buildings than was intended. Shortly afterwards the Scots abandoned the siege.

Dublin in The 16th Century

In 1537 a rebellion occurred in Dublin. The Lord Deputy of Ireland (The English kings deputy) was summoned to London. He appointed his son Vice-Deputy to rule in his absence. This young man was Lord

Fitzgerald. He heard that his father had been executed and angrily decided to rebel. He walked into the council chamber during a meeting and renounced his loyalty to the English king. He then left Dublin to gather support.

When he returned the Dubliners submitted and let him into the town but soldiers loyal to the king retreated into the castle and shut out the rebels. The rebels then murdered the Archbishop, which was a fatal mistake as it lost them public support. Fitzgerald sent a small number of men to besiege the castle then left Dublin to fight elsewhere. However the Dubliners turned against him and drove the men besieging the castle out of the town. Later Fitzgerald and his men returned to Dublin but this time they were shut out. They attempted to burn a gate but the Dubliners went out and drove the attackers off. Reinforcements arrived from England and the rebellion collapsed. Fitzgerald was later executed.

The Reformation happened peacefully in Dublin. When Henry VIII declared himself head of the church Dubliners actually celebrated. Henry closed the monasteries and nunneries, which caused some resentment but no actual rebellion. Henry also abolished the cult of relics but otherwise made few changes in religion. His son Edward and his daughter Elizabeth introduced more radical reforms but in Dublin and the rest of Ireland they were mostly ignored. Most people continued to practice the Old Catholic religion.

In the 16th century Dublin prospered. For the upper and middle classes there was an impressive rise in living standards. A writer said that they lived in houses 'so far exceeding their ancestors that they have thought rather to be another and new people than descendants of the old'. Previously most houses simply had a hole in the roof to let out smoke. In the 16th century chimneys became much more common. So did glass windows. Previously they were a luxury few people could afford.

Although conditions improved for the well off there were many beggars in Dublin. Many of them drifted in from the surrounding countryside. Furthermore Dublin was still dirty and unsanitary, like all 16th century towns. And it suffered from outbreaks of plague. One outbreak in 1579 killed thousands. Another tragedy in 1596 when a gunpowder store in Winetavern Street exploded. More than 120 people were killed.

In 1591 Queen Elizabeth granted a charter for a new university, Trinity College. The first students were admitted in 1594.

Dublin in The 17th Century

In 1604 Dublin was again visited by plague. Nevertheless Dublin continued to grow and may have had a population of around 20,000 by 1640.In 1616 Dublin gained its first street lighting when it was decreed that a candle or lantern should be hung outside every 5th house on dark nights. In 1621 a Custom House was built. In 1637 Dublin gained its first theater in Werburgh Street.

Following the English civil war of 1642-1646 Catholics were expelled from Dublin in large numbers, since their loyalty was suspect.

Plague broke out again in 1650. A large part of the population died, possibly as many as half. It was said at the time that Dublin was 'exceedingly depopulated'. In 1659 the population was less than 9,000. Nevertheless Dublin recovered and prospered in the late 17th century.

In 1662 Phoenix Park was laid out as a deer park. In the mid-18th century it became a popular place for walking. Meanwhile for centuries Dublin had only one bridge. A second one was built in 1670. The first newspaper in Dublin was produced in 1685.

Dublin continued to grow and many new houses were built. In 1670 a law forbade any new houses to have thatched roofs because of the danger of fire. The new houses were usually of brick with tiled roofs. Meanwhile in 1665 the Mayor of Dublin became a Lord Mayor and The Blue Coat School opened in 1669. It was rebuilt in 1773. The Tholsel, the town hall, was rebuilt in 1682 and a Royal Hospital for old soldiers was built in 1685. It is now the Irish Museum of Modern Art.

In the late 17th century the wool and linen trade with England grew. The industry was boosted by French Protestants who arrived in Dublin after fleeing from religious persecution.

Dublin in The 18th Century

By 1700 Dublin had about 60,000 inhabitants and it continued to grow rapidly. Conditions continued to improve in the 18th century, at least for the middle and upper classes. Dublin became a more refined and genteel city (for the well to do) but there was still a great deal of poverty.

Marsh's library was built in 1701 and in 1703 the Irish Parliament passed an act for building a workhouse where the destitute (of whom there were many) could be housed and fed. Then in 1711 Dublin gained its first fire brigade and St Anns Church was built in 1720. Dublin grew rapidly in the 18th century. Streets such as Aungier Street, Cuffe Street and Dawson Street were built early in the century. Merrion Square was built in 1762.

A number of hospitals were founded in the early 18th century. In 1729 a foundling hospital for unwanted children (of which there were many) opened in James Street. Jervis Hospital opened in 1721 Mercers Hospital was founded in 1734 by Mary Mercer. In 1745 St Patricks Hospital for the mentally ill was built and in 1752 Rotunda Maternity Hospital. In 1794 a dispensary was founded which gave free medicines to those too poor to buy them.

College Park was laid out in 1722. In the mid-18th century Phoenix Park became a fashionable place for the well to do to take walks.

Ranelagh Gardens opened in 1776. The Botanic Gardens were made in 1795. In the late 18th century St Stephens Green became a park.

Parliament House, a new meeting place for the Irish Parliament was built in 1735. Leinster House, which is the present home of the Irish Parliament was built in 1745 for the Duke of Leinster. A new Custom House was built in 1791. The Royal Exchange was built in 1779 and was later (1852) made the City Hall. In 1757 the Irish Parliament passed an act, which created a body of men with powers to widen the streets. In 1773 a body of men with power to pave, clean and light the streets of Dublin was formed. Their powers were transferred to the city council in 1851.

In the mid 18th century stagecoaches began running from Dublin to other towns such as Kilkenny, Cork and Belfast. There was a considerable coach making industry in the city. There were also many sedan chairs for the well to do and Grand canal opened in 1779. O'Connell Bridge was built in 1790.

In 1786 Dublin gained its first police force and Kilmainham prison was built in 1796. Meanwhile Guinness was first brewed in Dublin in 1759.

Dublin in The 19th Century

By 1800 the population of Dublin had risen to around 180,000. In 1803 and 1804 fever hospitals were opened in Dublin. The most common fever was typhus, sometimes called goal fever, because it was so common in jails. Lice spread typhus. Poor people frequently had lousy clothes. There was still a great deal of appalling poverty in the city with many families living in one room. In all European cities at the time there was terrible poverty but it seems to have been particularly bad in Dublin.

In the early 19th century several new bridges were built across the Liffey. O'Donovan Rossa bridge was built in 1813. Ha'penny Bridge (also called Liffey Bridge) opened in 1816 and Kingsbridge opened in 1828. (Its name was later changed to Heuston Bridge). Queen Victoria bridge, now Rory O'More Bridge, was built in 1859. The Royal Canal was opened in 1817. Meanwhile a column with a statue of Nelson on top was erected in 1808. It was destroyed in the 1960s. In 1825 St Marys Protestant Cathedral was built. However in 1855 the Dublin fair, which had been held in Dublin each year since the 13th century, was stopped.

Gradually during the 1800s conditions in Dublin improved. In 1824 a gasworks was built in Dublin and gas was used to light the streets from 1825. The first electric lights in Dublin were switched on in 1881 but electric light was a rare novelty until the early 20th century.

In the early 19th century sewers were laid but only in the middle class districts of Dublin (poor areas could not pay the necessary rates). But the sewers were extended in the 1850s, 1860s and 1870s. The railway reached Dublin in 1834 when a line to Kingsbridge was built. Horse drawn buses began running in Dublin in 1840. They were followed by horse drawn trams in 1872.

From 1838 there were workhouses in Dublin where the destitute were fed and housed. During the potato famine they were overwhelmed by the numbers fleeing starvation in the countryside. Soup kitchens had to be set up in the streets to try and feed them. Although the population of Ireland fell sharply after the famine the population of Dublin actually rose because of the number of starving people fleeing to the city.

Amenities in Dublin greatly improved in the 19th Century. In 1853 an industrial exhibition was held in Dublin on Leinster Lawn. Zoological Gardens opened in Phoenix Park in 1830. Portobello Gardens opened as a park in 1839. A Natural History Museum opened in 1857. The National Gallery of Ireland opened in 1864. In 1882 a memorial to O'Connell was erected in O'Connell Street. The Gaiety Theatre opened in 1871. The National Museum of Ireland opened in 1890.

The Catholic University in Dublin was founded in 1845. Catholics were allowed to attend Trinity College after 1873 but the Catholic Church disapproved of Catholics going there. Glasnevin Catholic cemetery opened in 1832. In 1892 a new fruit and vegetable market opened and in 1897 a new fish market opened.

Dublin in The 20th Century

On 24 April 1916 the Easter Rising took place in Dublin. The insurgents occupied the Post Office in O'Connell Street where their leader Patrick Pearse announced an Irish Republic. However the British crushed the rebellion and the insurgents surrendered on 29 April. The British then tried the insurgents and 15 of them were executed. Public opinion in Ireland was appalled and alienated by the executions.

However conditions in Dublin continued to improve during the 20th century. A new network of sewers was built in Dublin in 1892-1906. Butt Bridge was built in 1932. Talbot memorial bridge was built in 1978 and Frank Sherwin memorial bridge in 1982. East Link toll bridge was built in 1985. In the early 1990s a ring road was built around Dublin.

Meanwhile in 1904 Abbey Theatre was built. Gate Theatre followed in 1930. In 1907 the Irish International Exhibition was held in Herbert park. It was an exhibition of industrial and commercial goods. However in the early 20th century there was still appalling poverty in Dublin with perhaps a quarter of families living in one room. In 1912 slum demolition began when houses north of the Liffey were demolished and replaced with proper houses. Slum clearance on a large scale began in the 1930s and continued through the 1940s and 1950s.

In 1934 the Old Dublin Society was formed. In May 1941 the Germans bombed Dublin killing 28 people. Dublin Civic Museum opened in

1953. In 1962 the James Joyce Museum opened. In 1966 a Remembrance Garden was opened for all those who died in the fight for independence and the Friends of Medieval Dublin was founded in 1976.

In the 1960s and 1970s redevelopment of the city center took place, some of it controversial as it involved the demolition of fine old buildings. In the late 20th century the population of the city center fell as areas of slum housing were demolished and replaced by new estates on the outskirts of the city but in the 1990s new apartments were built in the city center. In the late 20th century traditional industries such as textiles, brewing and distilling declined but the city council built new industrial estates on the outskirts of the city and new industries like electronics, chemicals and engineering appeared.

In 1975 the Dublin Institute of Higher Education was formed. In 1990 it was made Dublin City University. The Catholic Church reversed its ban on Catholics attending Trinity College in 1970.

In 1988 Dublin celebrated its millennium. (Dublin was actually founded in 841 but in the year 988 an Irish king forced the townspeople to pay taxes to him. That year marks the beginning of Dublin as an Irish town). Also in 1988 Anna Livia Fountain was built in O'Connell Street. A statue of James Joyce was erected in Earl Street North in 1990. In 1985 a Jewish Museum opened in Dublin. In 1991 the Dublin Writers

Museum opened. Also in 1991 the Irish Museum of Modern Art opened.

After 1991 Temple Bar was renovated. The streets were pedestrianized and it now contains bars, shops, restaurants and art galleries. Furthermore George Bernard Shaw's birthplace in Dublin was opened to the public in 1993. Also in 1993 Dublinia, a Museum of Medieval Ireland opened. A Visitor Centre in the Custom House opened in 1997. Meanwhile Powerscourt Shopping Centre opened in 1981 in a house built in 1774. St Stephens Green Shopping Centre was built in the late 1980s and Jervis Street Shopping Centre opened in 1996.

Dublin in The 21st Century

In the 21st century Dublin continued to thrive. In 2000 a new pedestrian bridge, the Millennium Bridge was opened across the Liffey and in 2003 The Spire was erected. Trams returned to Dublin in 2004. The Convention Centre Dublin opened in 2010. Bord Gais Energy Theatre opened the same year, 2010. Today the population of Dublin is 527,000.

Tourism

Sightseeing

Dublin what to see. Complete travel guide

This city has an impressive history, wide choice of architectural places of interest and multiple entertainments. The southern part of Dublin is the most attractive for visitors of this magnificent city. Here you will find several ancient churches, visit Museum of History, or take a walk in old quarters that are stretched along the bank of the river.

The central street of Dublin is called O'Connell Street. This is home to numerous popular restaurants and bars. At night discos and night clubs are open and wait for their visitors. Temple Bar is known as the oldest region of the city. Tourists traditionally enjoy walking on its cozy shadowy streets, looking at houses that look very unusual for modern people. Among the fanciful houses you will find souvenir outlets and pubs, both decorated according to the style of previous centuries.

The main sight of Dublin is St Patrick's Cathedral that can be seen on the central square of Dublin. Many centuries ago here lived Saint Patrick. He organized christening of the locals and so many people gathered on the square to pray or to sanctify icons. Among interesting and memorable places in Dublin we should definitely mention Ely Place, Marriott Square, and Fitzwilliam Square. Many memorable obelisks are installed on these squares. Dublin Palace is the oldest building in the city. In was built in the 12th century. For a long time the palace was used as a summer residence of Irish kings. Later the palace was used as the residence of the British administration.

Among cultural facilities of Dublin we should definitely mention the National Theater of Ireland "Abbey", Dublin Civil Museum, State Concert Hall, National Gallery and several libraries opened over a hundred years ago. You should also definitely visit Trinity College that was founded by the order of the queen Elizabeth in the end of the 16th century. This is a beautiful architectural complex surrounded by old tress and amazing flowerbeds.

One of the busiest tourist places in the city is Grafton Street. Many beautiful historic buildings built in traditional style, have been preserved in it. The most popular souvenir shops of the city, and many other excellent national restaurants and bars, are located here too. This luxury street is one of the most expensive in the world in terms of rent and purchase of housing. There are several prestigious hotels located here.

One of the oldest buildings in the city is the "Christ Church Cathedral". It was built in the 11th century. Over hundreds of years of its existence, the facade of this historic building remained virtually unchanged, while its interior decoration was completely renovated during the last restoration in the 19th century. One of the main secrets of this picturesque cathedral is a cozy patio, decorated in a Victorian style.

There are many interesting museums in Dublin. One of the most unusual among them is the Guinness Storehouse. It is located in a historic building, which was one of the shops of the Guinness Brewery factory in the 8th century. This shop was closed in 1988. A few years after the closure of the shop, it was decided to open a museum in the large building. Its exposition is very multifaceted and is devoted to the history of brewing. Among the exhibits, one can also see old equipments from the factory.

The National Leprechauns Museum is a great place for a family visit. Its opening was in 2003. For Ireland, leprechauns are a true national symbol. During the excursion, visitors will be told a lot of interesting stories about these fabulous creatures.

Fans of theatrical art in Dublin, should visit the Abbey Theater. Its opening took place in 1904. However in 1951, the historical building of the theater was almost completely destroyed during a fire. Only 15 years later, was a new building constructed for the theater. Presently, the popular theater is largely focused on fans of contemporary art.

An intriguing sightseeing facility is the Kilmanchem Gaol. It was built in the 18th century and remained operational until the early 20th century. In this prison, many of the leaders of the Irish revolts were serving their sentences. In 1924, the Irish authorities decided to close it. Now the historic building is accessible to tourists. There are very interesting excursions here

A thousand years of history come alive in Dublin, where old and new rub shoulders. Take a stroll through Dublin's famous Georgian Squares dating back to the 17th century and soak up the atmosphere. At night, Dublin comes alive in its many theatres, music venues and cinemas. As many performing artists will tell you, a Dublin audience in full flight really raises the roof.

Dublin by Day

Discover Dublin By Bus: Dublin Bus Tours takes in most of the city centre sights. It is a 'hop-on, hop-off' affair, so you can get off the bus, take a look around and get a later bus to the next stop. A separate South Coast & Gardens Tour brings you through Sandycove and Dalkey to the Powerscourt stately home and estate in the Wicklow Mountains and back. The North Coast & Castle Tour brings you out to the fishing port of Howth and to Malahide Castle.

Dublin Castle: Dublin Castle stands right in the heart of historic Dublin. For more than 1,000 years it has been the symbolic stronghold for those who ruled Ireland, from the Vikings to the English. A sprawling complex of historic buildings as old as 934, it offers a unique crash course in Irish history.

Dublin Zoo: Situated in leafy Phoenix Park, Dublin Zoo is one of Ireland's most popular visitor attractions with close to one million visitors a year. Founded in 1830, it is the fourth oldest Zoo in Europe and offers an extensive selection of wild animals in carefully landscaped surroundings.

See Dublin From The Water: Experience Dublin on the water as well as on the road, travelling in a reconditioned American amphibian personnel carrier from World War II, a Dukw. The Viking Splash Tour takes in the sites of Viking Dublin, the city's two famous cathedrals (St. Patrick's and Christchurch), Trinity College, Government Buildings and Georgian Dublin. The water leg of the tour brings you to the recording studio of U2 and explores the newly developed Grand Canal Docklands. www.vikingsplash.ie

Guinness Storehouse: Located in the heart of the Guinness brewery, this hi tech visitor centre takes you through the 250 year history of The Dark Stuff. See, hear and smell how Guinness is made and take a complimentary pint in the Gravity Bar, the highest bar in Ireland. On a clear day you can enjoy an unrivalled view over the city and all along Dublin Bay from here! www.guinness-storehouse.com

Trinity College: Founded by Queen Elizabeth I, Trinity educated the elite of Anglo-Irish society for centuries. You can practically feel the wealth of its patrons standing in the Old Library or taking a stroll through the grounds. Trinity is literally a town within the town, complete with its own Cricket pitch. The renown Celtic art masterpiece, the illustrated Book of Kells is on display at Trinity. www.tcd.ie/visitors

National Museum Of Ireland: The National Museum has branches all over Dublin. Visit its Kildare Street buildings and prepare to get stunned by the sheer number and amazing beauty of its prehistoric gold ornaments which include the Ardagh Chalice and the famous Tara Brooch with their Celtic designs. www.museum.ie

Dublinia: Dublinia is an interactive exhibition taking you through Dublin in the Middle Ages. Play games in a medieval fair, walk through a rich merchant's townhouse or throw eggs (well, plastic balls) at an unlucky sod locked up in a stock. Great fun for children.www.dublinia.ie

Kilmainham Gaol: The guided tour of Europe's largest disused prison tells the tragic story behind Ireland's emergence as a modern nation. Built in 1792, Kilmaimham held many famous Irish Nationalists and Republicans from the Society of United Irishmen (1798) to the leaders of the 1916 Easter Rising, who were executed here. The prison was closed in 1924.www.heritageireland.ie

Irish Museum Of Modern Art: Housed in the former Royal Hospital Kilmainham, a 17th century home for ex-soldiers, the IMMA stages state of the art exhibitions of international artists and has a collection of Irish contemporary art that is a must see. Don't forget to step outside, check out the amazing Georgian architecture and discover the 17th century maze in the ornamental gardens! www.modernart.ie

Hugh Lane Gallery: This elegant town house on Parnell Square houses an eclectic collection of French Impressionists - including works by Monet, Manet and Degas - and Irish art from the 19th-21st century. The gallery contains Dublin-born painter Francis Bacon's full-size studio, which was brought here piece by piece from London after his death in 1992. www.hughlane.ie

National Botanic Gardens: Partake in a great Northside tradition and take a stroll through Botanic Gardens on a Sunday afternoon. It is free, and if the weather is with you, there are few places more relaxing. A lovely little spot that is off the beaten tourist track. www.botanicgardens.ie

Casino Marino: Hidden away in a quiet suburb, this gem of Palladian architecture in Ireland is well worth a visit. The first Earl of Charlemont had the Casino built as a venue for intimate dinner parties, literary circles and the odd game of cards - all very discretely out of sight from his main house further down the hill. He even built a tunnel for his servants to come up from the kitchens of the main house without being seen or spoiling the guests' view over Dublin Bay. www.heritageireland.ie

Temple Bar Market: Slurp some fresh Irish Oysters, sample Irish charcuterie and farm cheeses or just drift along with the crowds at this ever popular Saturday foodies market in the middle of Temple Bar. The market is held every Saturday from approximately 10:00-16:30 in Meeting House Square. www.templebar.ie

Science Gallery: Located next door to Trinity College, Dublin's newest attraction is a cutting edge museum and gallery devoted to modern science. Far from being a haven for technology nerds, the gallery focuses on the possibilities scientific progress opens for the arts and our everyday lives. www.sciencegallery.ie

Dublin Writers Museum: Many famous novelists, poets and playwrigths were born in Dublin and had their formative experiences here. If there is a literary style that can be closely associated with Dublin, it has to be down to earth, populist with good plots and lashings of satyrical humour.The most famous Dublin writers are probably Jonathan Swift, Bram Stoker, Oscar Wilde, James Joyce and George Bernard Shaw. The Dublin Writers Museum tells you more about the lives these famous authors led and introduces you to some lesser known, but no less interesting writers. www.writersmuseum.com

Dublin Bus

There are several different types of buses on Dublin's roads. Dublin Bus (Bus Átha Cliath in Gaelic) with its fleet of yellow and blue liveried single and double-deckers gets you around town and to and from the suburbs. The white Bus Eireann coaches with the orange greyhound logo on the side connect you with other main Irish cities.

Tourist hop-on hop-off bus

An open top double decker bus will make sightseeing entertaining without having to go through the hassle of daily city life. These busses go around Dublins highlights in 8 to 20 minute intervals and you can get on and off as many times as you like. Meet fellow tourists and share your impressions.

Getting Around Dublin By Bus

Dublin Bus (Bus Átha Cliath) is the main public transport provider. Its fleet of yellow and blue liveried buses carries 70% of all peak time public transport, which equals roughly half a million customers a day.

Bus Stops And Timetables

Bus stops are marked by a yellow pole crowned with a small yellow disc bearing the blue Dublin Bus logo. Distances between stops can vary significantly. In the city centre, they are usually quite close together. It is not unusual for a bus to stop every 150-200 metres on some routes.

If there is a timetable at your stop, take it as an indication of services only. The traffic in Dublin is quite heavy, particularly during rush hour from 7:00-9:00 and 16:00-19:00. There are some dedicated bus lanes, but they can mainly be found outside the city centre proper. If you are in a hurry, please factor this in and allow ample time to reach your destination.

Dublin Bus Fares

In Dublin you pay the driver. Fares are calculated in stages, the more stages between your starting point and your destination the higher the fare. A typical city centre journey will cost you approximately €1.60 (€0.80 for children under 16). The maximum fare is €4.50.

Some bus stops have tables displaying fares to different destinations from that particular stop. However, most bus stops don't divulge that sort of detail and Dubliners usually just state their destination and the driver will name the fare.

Make sure you have plenty of small change. Dublin Bus drivers are not required to accept notes and might refuse to let you on board. If you do not have the exact fare you will not get change from the driver. Instead, your ticket has a section that says 'Refund' and states the appropriate amount. If you want your change back, you need to head to the Dublin Bus office at 59 Upper O'Connell Street.

Rambler Ticket

If you plan to make more than the odd journey on the bus during your visit to Dublin you should consider purchasing a Rambler Ticket. They are available for one day, three days, five days and seven days. A one day adult Rambler Ticket costs €6.00, a family ticket costs €10.00. Day tickets can be bought from the bus driver. You can buy longer term tickets online on the Dublin Bus homepage.www.dublinbus.ie

Dublin Bus Etiquette

Dubliners queue at the bus stop, with the person who was there first nearest to the stop sign. If your stop services more than one bus line it is pefectly fine to jump the queue when the person in front of you is obviously not waiting for your bus. You enter and leave a bus through the front door by the driver only. You will notice many passengers muttering a 'thank you' to the driver when leaving the bus. If your bus has a middle door, do not bother to queue up in front of it, your driver will most likely not open it and you have to face a mad dash to the front of the bus to make your stop.

Going Long Distance

Bus Eireann coaches start and terminate at the Busaras or central bus terminal at Store Street on the North Quays near the International Financial Services Centre. Apart from connecting you with all major cities in Ireland, Bus Eireann also offers day trips to locations near Dublin, such as the megalithic tombs at Newgrange and the early Christian monastery and picturesque mountain lakes at Glendalough. Please.

Dublin Castle

Dublin Castle is situated in the very heart of historic Dublin. For more than 700 years, from 1200 until the formation of the Irish Republic in 1921, it was the centre of the English colonial administration in Ireland. A sprawling complex of historic buildings from between 930 and 1830, it offers a unique crash course in Irish history.

Dublin Castle's History

In 930, the Vikings built fortifications at the junction of the River Liffey and its tributary, the now underground River Poddle. The site was called Dubh Linn in Gaelic (pronounced Dub Lin), which means Black Water.

When the Normans invaded Dublin in 1169, they picked Dublin Castle as their stronghold. The first 'castle' in the proper sense of the word - stone walls and ditches - was completed by the English in 1230. The Great Courtyard of today corresponds closely with these fortifications, with the Record Tower as the last intact medieval tower of Dublin. The tower served as a high security prison in Tudor times.

Dublin Castle was the dungeon for state prisoners and the seat of Parliament, which met in the Great Hall before the hall burnt down in the great fire of 1684 and Parliament moved to College Green in 1731. The Courts of Law and the Court of Exchequer also met at Dublin Castle. The Castle further housed the repository of the Royal Treasury and the Royal Mint, army and police barracks, armaments factories and weapons stores.

As a symbol of English reign, Dublin Castle was a key target during the Easter Rising of 1916, which marked the first step towards the end of British rule in Ireland. One of the first fatalities of the Rising was a policeman named O'Brien, who attempted to shut the Castle's Cork Hill Gate on an advancing rebel party. Captain Séan Connolly who fired the shot was killed by army snipers located on the roof of Bedford Tower when he attempted to raise the rebel flag on adjacent City Hall.

Dublin Castle Opening Times

You are free to wander around Dublin Castle, but if you like to take a peek inside some of the more splendid buildings you will need to join a guided tour. Tours are held Mondays to Friday between 10:00 and 16:45 and Saturdays and Sundays from 14:00-16:45.

Dublin Castle Prices

A Guided tour taking in the State Apartments, Undercroft and Chapel Royal costs €4.50 for Adults and €2.00 for Children under 12.

Chester Beatty Library

The Chester Beatty Library on the ground of Dublin Castle is renowned for its outstanding collection of Asian and Middle Eastern art. The Library's collection includes manuscripts, prints, icons, miniature paintings, early printed books and objects d'art from Asia, the Middle East, North Africa and Europe. Entry to the CBL is free. Opening times are Tue-Friday from 10-17, sat 11-17 and Sun 13-17. From May-September, the library also opens on Mondays from 10-17.

Garda Museum

The museum of the Irish police force, the Garda, is located in the 13th century Record Tower. Entry is free. Opening times are Monday to Friday from 9:30-16:30.

Revenue Museum

The Revenue Museum is situated in the Crypt of the Chapel Royal. The museum focuses on smuggling, taxes and duties in Ireland through the centuries. Entry is free. Opening times are Monday to Friday from 9:00-16:00.

Getting To Dublin Castle

Dublin Castle can be reached by an easy 10 minute walk from Temple Bar or Grafton Street. Dublin Busroutes 77/77A, 56A and 49 from Eden Quay and the 123 from O'Connell Street all stop at Dublin Castle's Palace Street Gate.

Dublin ZOO

Situated in leafy Phoenix Park, Dublin Zoo is one of Ireland's most popular visitor attractions with close to one million visitors a year. In Dublin, it certainly counts among the Top Three attractions, together with Trinity College and the Guinness Storehouse brewery museum. From arctic fox to zebra, Dublin Zoo offers an extensive selection of wild animals in carefully landscaped surroundings.

Zoo History

Dublin Zoo is the fourth oldest zoo in Europe. It was opened in 1830 by the Zoological Society of Dublin. The animals were initially supplied by London Zoo, which had opened its doors only four years earlier. Only the zoos in Vienna and Paris are older, dating back to 1752 and 1793 respectively.

And here is a bit of macabre history for you: During the Easter Rising of 1916, zoo workers were unable to get out of Phoenix Park. When meat supplies for the animals ran out, zoo workers decided to kill other animals in the zoo to keep the more valuable lions and tigers alive.

Dublin Zoo Today

Dublin Zoo has been registering rising visitor figures over the past few years. Dublin Zoo's popularity is particularly linked to its successful breeding programme. A series of rare births, such as those of a bull Elephant, a Rhinoceros, a Californian Sealion and a Tapir in 2008 attracted a total of 932,000 visitors, an impressive increase of 30,000 visitors compared to the previous year. The signs are set for this trend to continue. The first birth of 2009 was a female Giraffe calf on 4th January.

The Zoo is constantly updating its animals' habitats. At time of going to press, the African Plains are undergoing re-development to improve living conditions for the Zoo's herd of White Rhinos among other

Animals from the African grasslands. The African Plains have been recently re-opened.

Zoo Prices

Admission prices are €15.00 for Adults and €10.50 for Children under 16. Children under three visit for free. You can purchase various size family tickets. A Family Ticket for two Adults and two Children costs €43.50, for instance.

Dublin Zoo spends approximately 10% of its annual surplus on various research and conservation projects benefiting animals in the wild.

Zoo Opening Times

During the main season from March to September, Dublin Zoo opens daily from 9:30 to 18:00. The extensive African Plains area closes half an hour before the rest of the Zoo, giving you ample time to make your way back to the central area. Closing times in the Winter and Autumn months vary, depending on lighting conditions, from 17:30 in October to 16:00 in November and December.

How to Get To Dublin Zoo

Dublin Zoo is located at the Parkgate Street end of Phoenix Park on the Northside of the city. The Zoo is approximately a 20 minutes walk away from Heuston Station. Alternatively you can take the bus number 90 from Heuston to Phoenix Park. The Red Luas tram line gets you from the O'Connell Street area to Heuston Station. The Zoo is well served by bus from most areas in Dublin. Lines convenient for the Zoo are 10/10A, 25/25A, 26, 66/66A, 67/67A, 68 and 69. There is a free car park off Lord's Walk behind the Zoo.

Guinness Storehouse Dublin

What could be more quintessentially Dublin than visiting the home of Guinness, the dark, malty beer that is exported from Dublin's fair city to virtually everywhere in the World.

First Impressions

The Guinness Storehouse on the grounds of the actual, working Guinness brewery takes you on an interactive trip through the brewing process. Feel the heat, smell the grains and hear the din of the machinery. When you're finished, head for the Gravity Bar on the top floor which boasts the highest bar in Dublin and the best 360 degree views of the city.

As a tourist attraction, the Guinness Storehouse ranks among the Top 3 in Dublin, together with the Zoo and Trinity College. And it is easy to see why, once you set a foot in the door. The massive red brick building from 1904 has been completely gutted revealing its futuristic steel beam structure. If you look closely, the way the beams have been exposed resembles a giant pint glass with the Gravity Bar as its head!

A Brief History Of Guinness

The sprawling St. James Gate brewery is like a city within the city of Dublin. A forward looking businessman, founder Arthur Guinness took out a 9,000 year lease of the premises in 1759 for a rent of £45 a year. Guinness stout with its characteristic black body, creamy head and malty flavour was first brewed by Arthur Guinness in the 1770s and quickly became the brewery's top product. Wisely, Arthur switched all production to stout in 1799.

Today, Guinness stout is sold in some 150 countries throughout the World and the company estimates that some 10 million glasses of 'the dark stuff' are consumed every day around the globe.

Storehouse History

Built in 1904 following the example of the Chicago school of architecture, the Storehouse was where grains, water, malted barley, hops and yeast were left to ferment to make Guinness until as recently as 1988. Now the place combines sleek high tech looks with early industrial architecture for a very cool effect.

Bars And Food At The Storehouse

This being a working brewery, you have a choice of three bars: The Brewery Bar, the Source Bar and the Gravity Bar. Make sure you visit the Gravity Bar for the view over Dublin and the complimentary pint of Guinness, which is included in your ticket price. If you are feeling hungry, head for the Brewery Bar on the fifth floor, which serves food throughout the day. If you want to get away from the crowds for a quiet pint of Guinness, try the Source Bar, also located on the fifth floor.

The Guinness Flagship Store

On the ground floor of the Guinness Storehouse you will find the single largest display of Guinness branded goodies in all of Ireland, possibly even the World. From lovingly made replicas of 20th century advertising signs and Guinness glasses to t-shirts, fleeces and other apparel with the characteristic Guinness logo you can buy a host of uniquely Irish presents at the Guinness flagship store.

Opening Times And Prices

The Guinness Storehouse is open seven days a week from 9:30 to 17:00. During July and August, the Storehouse stays open until 19:00.

Adult tickets include a complimentary pint in the Gravity Bar and cost €15.00 per person. Book online and you get a 10% discount, which brings the price down to €13.50 per adult. Admission for children costs €5.00 and there are further discounts for families, students and senior citizens.

How To Get To The Guinness Storehouse

The Guinness Storehouse is located in Market Street, just off James's Street. You can take the Red Luas from the city centre in the direction of Tallaght and get off in James's Street. It's a five minute walk from the Luas stop to the Storehouse.

Bus routes 123 from O'Connell Street and Dame Street or 78a and 51b from Aston Quay all stop close to the Storehouse. Ask the bus driver when you get on to give you a shout when the stop for the Guinness Storehouse comes up!

If you are travelling by car, there is complimentary parking for Storehouse visitors on Crane Street.

If you are good on foot, the weather is fair and you are feeling adventurous, you can walk from the city centre to the Guinness Storehouse in half an hour. The surroundings of the Storehouse include some of the oldest and least changed parts of Dublin, so it is quite an interesting walk.

Trinity College Dublin

Trinity College is Ireland's oldest university. It was founded by Queen Elizabeth I in 1592. Due to its picturesque setting and the famous people connected with it - Oscar Wilde studied here - Trinity College is one of the city's main tourist attractions. The Trinity library harbours the world's most famous early medieval manuscript, the Book Of Kells. Trinity's campus is located in the centre of Dublin and its impressive 47 acres feature cricket and rugby pitches as well as tennis courts.

History Of Trinity College

As one of the oldest universities in the British Isles, Trinity College is a symbol for the importance of Dublin as an economic and political powerhouse in Elizabethan times. Originally set up in 1592 for the education of the protestant elite, Trinity opened its doors to Catholics in 1793. The college first admitted women to its courses in 1904. The majority of buildings on the Trinity campus date from the 18th century, when a significant building programme created the elegant yet understated look that is now synonymous with the Dublin university.

Trinity College Today

Trinity College is the only Irish university to rank in the top 100 world universities and amongst the top 50 European universities, as rated by UK newspaper The Times. More than 15,000 students were registered at Trinity College in the 2007-08 academic year. More than 82,500 Trinity alumni were spread over the globe by early 2009. The university's annual Trinity Ball is one of Dublin's major social events and ranks among the most lavish student nights in Europe.

The Book Of Kells

The most precious single item on the Trinity campus is undoubtedly the Book of Kells. The book is an illuminated manuscript from 800AD which is housed in the Old Library building of the university. The manuscript contains the four gospels of the New Testament. It is the imaginative use of figures and complex ornaments to highlight the first letter on a page that makes the Book Of Kells so special. Incredibly vivid and colourful even 1,200 years after they were drawn by monks, these illuminated letters have come to define much of what we know these days as Celtic style. A librarian turns over a new page of The

Book Of Kells every day. SO if you come here for a year, you would get to see the entire manuscript. Alternatively, you can buy the Book Of Kells on DVD. It is a must have for anybody interested in graphic design, typography or medieval art.

The Old Library

Apart from the Book Of Kells, the Old Library is worth a visit for its magnificent Main Chamber. The 65 metres long hall houses 200,000 of Trinity's oldest books. With its ancient wooden shelves, alcoves and vaulted ceiling it looks just like a picture perfect library. Also on display in the Old Library at Trinity is one of the dozen or so remaining copies of the 1916 Proclamation of the Irish Republic, which was read out aloud by Patrick Pearse outside the General Post Office on 24 April 1916 at the start of the Easter Rising.

The Old Library at Trinity College is open Monday to Saturday from 9:30 to 17:00 and Sundays from 9:30 to 16:30. In the winter months, the Old Library opens at 12:00 noon on Sundays. On Irish Bank Holidays, the library usually stays open from 9:30 to 17:00. The entry for adults is €9.00, children under 12 years of age go for free. Concessions for families, students, senior citizens are available.

Douglas Hyde Gallery

The Douglas Hyde Gallery is located adjacent to the Nassau Street gate into Trinity College campus. The gallery's stark, modernist architecture is a fitting frame to the cutting edge contemporary art exhibited on its two floors. The Douglas Hyde Gallery has no permanent collection. Instead, exhibitions change frequently to reflect trends in contemporary arts. The Douglas Hyde Gallery is open Mondays to Fridays from 11:00 to 18:00, Thursdays from 11:00 to 19:00 and Saturdays until 16:45. The gallery is closed on Sundays. Entry to the Douglas Hyde Gallery is free of charge.

Oscar Wilde Centre

The Oscar Wilde Centre is a resource centre for international and Irish writers interested in developing their knowledge of Irish literature. The centre offers a M.Phil degree in Irish Writing and an M. Phil in Creative Writing. The centre is located at the former Wilde family home on 21 Westland Row, adjacent to the Trinity campus.

Science Gallery

Dublin's newest visitor attraction is the Science Gallery, which opened its doors in February 2008 on two floors of the Naughton Institute on the Trinity College campus. Exhibitions typically feature hands on visitor participation and are great fun for kids and adults alike. Initially, Trinity College expected to attract 50,000 visitors to its newest public attraction in the first year. The Science Gallery proved more popular than expected, with some 120,000 curious sightseers flocking to its exhibitions.

Samuel Beckett Theatre

The Samuel Beckett Theatre is the campus theatre of Trinity College's

Department of Drama. During term time, the theatre showcases works by the Department and its courses. In the summer months and during breaks, the theatre's stage hosts visiting dance and theatre companies from all over Europe, Japan and the United States. The Samuel Beckett Theatre also participates in the Dublin Fringe Festival and the Dublin Theatre Festival.

Walking Tours Of The Campus

Trinity College offers walking tours of its historic campus during the summer months. Tours depart from a desk located in the Main Gate of the College and last approximately 30 minutes. The tour will give you an overview of the history of Trinity College, its architecture, its most famous graduates and includes an optional visit to the Old Library and the Book of Kells. The campus tour on its own costs €5.00 per person; together with a visit to the Old Library you pay €10.00. Tours depart every 40 minutes between 10:15 and 15:40 from mid-May to September.

Campus Accommodation

Trinity College offers hostel accommodation during the summer months from mid June to September. Trinity's 800 rooms are mostly located in the most historic areas of the campus with many buildings dating back to the 17th and 18th century. Rooms are priced to appeal to the budget traveller, yet most of the rooms are overlooking the picturesque Trinity campus.

How To Get To Trinity College Dublin

Trinity College is located just off the Northern end of Grafton Street, with the main gate located at College Green and side gates on Nassau Street, Lincoln Place and Pearse Street. The closest Dart stop for Trinity College is Pearse station, which is convenient for both the Pearse Street and Lincoln Place entrances. The 128 bus goes from the Connolly stop on the Red Luas line to Nassau Street, a five minute walk away from the university. The 92 bus brings you from Heuston station to Trinity College. The 123 bus from Dame Street/O'Connell Street stops at College Green, opposite the main gate to Trinity College.

National Museum of Ireland

If you want to discover some of Ireland's secrets you need to visit the National Museum of Ireland. Did you know, for instance, that some of the richest ancient gold treasures in Europe were found in Ireland and date back as much as 4,200 years?

The National Museum Of Ireland has split its extensive collection into two main themes: Archeaology focuses on Ireland's rich Celtic heritage and Decorative Arts & History examines the vibrant role of Ireland throughout modern history. The Archaeology Museum and the Decorative Arts & History Museum are both conveniently located in the city centre of Dublin and worth a visit.

Archaeology

The National Museum Of Ireland's Archaeology branch in Dublin hosts one of the largest exhibitions of prehistoric gold jewellery in Europe. The unique, abstract designs on these pieces include some of the most breath-taking examples of ancient Celtic art.

Huge, crescent shaped neck collars or 'lunulae', chunky bracelets and substantial dress-fasteners make up the largest part of the jewellery pieces on display. Gold was hammered paper thin or shaped into solid bars and elegantly twisted.

The craftsmanship is amazing, particularly when you consider that the oldest pieces in the collection date back to 2200BC, the 'youngest' artefacts are from 500BC.

Opening Times And Prices

The Archaeology branch of the National Museum is open Tuesday to Saturday from 10:00 to 17:00 and Sunday from 14:00 to 17:00. Admission to the museum is free.

How To Get To The National Museum of Ireland - Archaeology

The Archaeology museum is within easy walking distance from Trinity College, the Grafton Street main shopping area, St Stephen's Green and most city centre hotels. It is literally only a short five minute walk from either Trinity or St Stephen's Green to the National Museum's Archaeology building on Kildare Street. You can take the Green Luas to

St Stephen's Green and walk, or you can take bus 7, 7a, 10, 11 or 13 from O'Connell Street.

Decorative Arts & History

Ireland's influence on the Western World as we know it is often overlooked. The National Museum of Ireland - Decorative Arts & History highlights some of the contributions Ireland made throughout the centuries

From Irish mercenaries in various wars in Europe and the Americas, the Irish Brigades, to modernist 20th century designer Eileen Gray, the National Museum has many fascinating stories to tell.

Gray created iconic furniture in the 1920s and 1930s such as the adjustable chrome table 'E-1027' and the 'Bibendum' chair. At the height of her fame, Gray was asked by Le Corbusier to exhibit in his pavilion at the Paris World Fair in 1937.

The museum's choice of exhibits is eclectic and never dull. Housed in the impressive grounds of former army barracks, the Collins Barracks, the museum is situated on the quays of the River Liffey.

Opening Times And Prices

The Decorative Arts & History branch of the National Museum is open to the public from Tuesday to Saturday, 10:00 to 17:00, and on Sunday from 14:00 to 17:00. Admission to the museum is free. Special events and guest exhibitions may carry a small charge.

How To Get To The National Museum of Ireland Decorative Arts & Design

The Decorative Arts & History museum is located at Collins Barracks in Benburb Street. The Red Luas line's 'Museum' stop is right outside the main gate. Heuston Station is literally across the river from the museum and you can walk between the two in less than 10 minutes. From the city centre, you can take bus 90 from Aston Quay or buses 25, 25a, 66 and 67 from Wellington Quay.

Dublinia and the Viking World

Dublinia shows you firsthand what it was like to live in Dublin at the time of the Vikings and in the middle ages up to the beginning 16th century. It is a highly interactive museum full of atmospheric 3-d displays and with many hands on activities for visitors.

Dublinia In Action

Stroll through a medieval market and visit a rich merchant's house. You can wear medieval clothes, throw rotten eggs and veg (well, soft plastic balls) at a criminal locked up in the pillories and try your luck at fun fair games. Or why not try on some medieval armour and find out what weight the knights actually had to carry around with them?

Don't be shy. It's great fun for kids and adults with a sense of humour. All exhibits come with plain-English explanations that give you a taste for the time even if history is not usually your thing.

The Viking World

After you survived the Middle Ages, delve deeper and experience life in the times of the Vikings. See for yourself how much space you had as a crew member on a Viking long ship, learn to write in Viking Runes and listen to long Sagas recited by an elder while you are sitting around the camp fire. Again, it's an absolute blast for children and open minded adults.

St Michael's Tower

This 17th century cut stone tower offers great views over Dublin and the River Liffey from its top platform. There are signs pointing out the major landmarks you can see from here, weather permitting. The interior of the tower is quite impressive, with just a metal staircase snaking its way up and the lack of floors giving you full view of the majestic height of the structure. It's a steep climb of 96 steps to get to the viewing platform. You don't want to be suffering from vertigo here and high heels are not the best choice of footwear for the climb.

The History Of Dublinia

Dublinia is located in a 19th century neo-Gothic building that housed the Synod Hall of the Church Of Ireland until 1983. The building was erected on the site of an older, 17th century church of which only the bell tower survived. The tower is now part of the Dublinia museum. The building is connected with historic Christchurch Cathedral on the opposite side of St Michael's Hill via an enclosed pedestrian bridge.

The museum opened its doors in 1993 and added its permanent exhibition The Viking World in 2005.

Opening Times

Dublinia is open daily March to September: 10am - 6.30pm (last entry 5.30pm) and from October to February 10am -5.30pm (last entry 4.30pm).

Prices

Tickets cost €8.50 for adults and €5.50 for children. There are further discounts available for families, students and senior citizens.

How To Get To Dublinia

Dublinia is located on St Michael's Hill, opposite Christchurch Cathedral. The 123 bus from O'Connell Street or Dame Street stops on High Street in view of the Dublinia building. Just walk back 100 metres on High Street and turn left, walking down St Michael's Hill towards the River Liffey. The entrance to Dublinia is to your left.

Irish Museum of Modern Art, Dublin

Marvel at this fabulous collection of modern art in the oldest showpiece building in Dublin. There are few places in Dublin where the old and the new are so strikingly in balance. The Irish Museum of Modern Art in the impressive 17th century Royal Hospital Kilmainham is well worth a visit.

Stunning Location: The Royal Hospital Kilmainham

Sparked by the construction of Les Invalides in Paris under Louis XIV, Dublin build its own home for war veterans in 1684. Closely following the French blueprint, the Royal Hospital Kilmainham has four wings enclosing a courtyard with covered walks. Formal 17th century gardens with an elaborate maze surround the Hospital.

At the time, the Hospital was the first monumental public building to be erected in Dublin. Others, such as the Custom House and the Four Courts followed, but the Hospital well and truly marks the beginning of Dublin's love affair with spectacular architecture during its Georgian economical heyday.

The Museum's Art Collections

The Irish Museum Of Modern Art (IMMA) opened its doors in 1991. IMMA's collection contains some 4,500 works from the 1940's onwards. The museum's permanent collection is 1,650 works strong. Collections on loan, such as the Musgrave Kinley Outsider Art Collection and the Weltkunst Foundation Collection of British Art from the 1980s and 1990s make up the rest. IMMA also houses the Madden Arnholz Collection of prints by Old Masters.

The museum hosts regular exhibitions bringing the oeuvre of international avantgarde artists into the intimate Dublin setting. Recent highlights include exhibitions of works by Laurie Anderson, Keith Haring and William S. Burroughs among others.

Opening Times And Prices

The Irish Museum Of Modern Art is open from 10:00-17:00, except for Mondays, when it closes at 15:00. On Sundays and public holidays, the museum opens at 12:00 noon. Admission to the museum is generally free. Some guest exhibitions or events may carry a small charge.

How To Get To The Museum Of Modern Art

The Royal Hospital Kilmainham and the Irish Museum Of Modern Art are located opposite Heuston Station on the South bank of the River Liffey. You can take the Red Luas to Heuston and walk up the hill in front of the station. It's a fairly easy 10 minute walk. Alternatively, take bus routes 123 from O'Connell Street or Dame Street, 51 or 78A from Aston Quay in the city centre or the 90 from Connolly Station or Tara Street Dart Station.

Hugh Lane Gallery, Dublin

Contrasting the old with the new, the Hugh Lane Gallery shows works by contemporary Irish and international artists next to Impressionist masterworks and other 19th century art. The original collection, donated by the Gallery's founder Sir Hugh Lane, is constantly updated.

History Of The Gallery

The Hugh Lane Gallery can claim to be the first public museum of modern art in the world! Irish-born art dealer Sir Hugh Lane found fame and fortune in London in the 19th century. Fascinated by the

Irish art scene at the beginning of the 20th century, Sir Hugh founded the Municipal Gallery Of Modern Art in Dublin in 1908.

The original gallery was located off St Stephens Green in Harcourt Street and has since been re-named and moved to Charlemont House, the opulent Georgian town house of the Earl Of Charlemont on Parnell Square at the top of O'Connell Street.

The Hugh Lane Gallery's Collection

The gallery has expanded Sir Hugh's collection considerably over the years and currently owns some 2,000 outstanding works of art. The collection focuses predominantly on 19th century paintings and sculpture and contains Impressionist masterpieces by artists including Manet, Monet, Renoir and Degas.

A busy schedule of exhibitions by contemporary artists introduces more radical takes on art. Don't be surprised to walk through the old fashioned rooms to suddenly stumble across a cluster of multimedia installations.

Contrasts are what makes the Hugh Lane Gallery so enjoyable.

Francis Bacon's Studio

His huge canvases of decomposing faces and contorted bodies made Francis Bacon on of Dublin's most famous sons. Born in Dublin's Baggot Street in 1909, Bacon moved to London in 1929 and saw his star - and prices for his paintings - rising in the late 1940's.

After Bacon's death in 1992, the Hugh Lane Gallery bought the entire contents of the artist's South Kensington studio - From piles of old newspapers to unfinished paintings. The lovingly reconstructed studio is now encased in plexiglass and offers a fascinating glimpse into Bacon's grungy and chaotic world. Bacon's studio at the Hugh Lane is a must for fans of 20th century art.

Opening Times And Prices

The Hugh Lane Gallery is open Tuesdays to Thursdays from 10:00-18:00, Fridays and Saturdays from 10:00-17:00 and on Sundays from 11:00-17:00. The gallery is closed on Mondays. The Hugh Lane Gallery is funded by the City of Dublin and entry is free of charge. Some guest exhibitions and events may carry a small charge.

How To Get To The Hugh Lane Gallery

Located on Parnell Square at the Northern end of O'Connell Street, tucked away behind the Rotunda Hospital, the Hugh Lane Gallery is only a short walk away from many bus routes. The 3,7,10,11,13,16, 19, 46A and 123 all stop within a five minutes' walk of the gallery.

The Hugh Lane Gallery Address

Charlemont House

Parnell Square (North)

Dublin 1, Ireland

National Botanic Gardens, Dublin

The National Botanic Gardens celebrate their bicentennial in 2009. The gardens were first opened in 1809, barely 50 years after Kew Gardens in London. Like Kew Gardens, Dublin boasts a number of spectacular Victorian glasshouses.

The Botanic Gardens Today

The Botanic Gardens contain 15,000 plant species from all around the world. The real pleasure you will derive from visiting the gardens is the feeling of immense calm and relaxation you take home after a stroll here. It's a small enough place for an easy walk. Generations of Dubliners have come out here for a 'constitutional', particularly after a roast beef or lamb lunch on Sundays.

On a sunny day, you can immerse yourself into the positively cheerful holiday atmosphere of couples and families strolling around the gardens.

If that sounds too wholesome, then check out the many sculptures which are generally dotted around the gardens or visit the palm house or the reassuringly down-to-earth vegetable gardens.

Refreshments At The Botanic Gardens

Please note that, despite the otherwise relaxed atmosphere, picnics are not exactly welcome here. But a cafeteria with a mouth-watering range of cream cakes and other treats invites those of you with a sweet tooth for a refuel stop after all that exertion of walking through the flowerbeds and rose gardens.

Opening Times And Prices

It's hard to believe, but entry to the Botanic Gardens is free! The gardens are open to the public all year round and only close on Christmas Day. The opening times are 9:00-18:00 from February to November and 9:00 to 16:30 during the rest of the year.

How To Get To The National Botanic Gardens

The National Botanic Gardens are located in the picturesque suburb of Glasnevin, roughly 3.5 km north of the city centre. Take bus 19 or 19a from O'Connell Street. The bus stops outside the main gate to the gardens.

Casino Marino, Dublin

Imagine a classical looking building where nothing is what it seems. Casino Marino is a lovingly restored 18th century pleasure house full of optical illusions.

The Casino's Secrets

Walking up to the Casino you first notice that you can't look into the windows. From whatever angle you look at them, the windows remain black. That's because each individual pane is skilfully bevelled to deflect the light. The massive columns are hollow and serve as gutters and the decorative urns on the roof are actually chimneypots.

Step inside and you will find that what looks like a small garden pavilion actually hides 16 rooms on three floors, including kitchens and servants quarters, a library, several reception rooms and bedrooms.

The History Of The Casino

The Casino is a masterpiece of Palladian architecture in Europe, possibly one of the finest outside Italy. Inspired by the Roman temples and the Palladian villas he saw on his tour of Italy, James Caulfeild, the first Earl of Charlemont, instructed architect Sir William Chambers to draw up the plans for a Casino, or 'little house' in Italian.

The 'little house' was never inhabited; it served as an impressive folly to entertain the Earl's friends. Servants would bring up food supplies and wine from the Earl's main house through a tunnel, completely out of view of the guests.

Being the Earl's guest at the Casino was not without dangers in the 1700s. The house was located fairly isolated on pastures roamed by highwaymen and the Earl Charlemont kept armed bodyguards on the premises to fend off unwanted gate crashers.

It is a truly fascinating trip to a Dublin long gone, barely a 20 minutes bus ride north from the centre of town. Take the guided tour to see the inside of the Casino and listen to the colourful tales of the guides.

Prices And Opening Times

The Casino can be accessed from April to September between 10:00 and 18:00. You can walk around the grounds for free but to get inside the building you need to join a guided tour. Tours take approximately one hour and cost €3.00 for adults and €1.00 for children. Maybe it's because of the unusual nature of the building, maybe it's because the Casino is off the beaten track, but the guides here are some of the most knowledgeable and enthusiastic in all of Dublin's many public attractions.

How To Get To The Casino Marino

The Casino is located on the Northside in the suburb of Marino, just off the Malahide Road, close to the junction with Griffith Avenue. Take the Dart to Clontarf station and walk up Malahide Road or take the 123 bus from O'Connell Street to the end of Griffith Avenue, turn left and walk up the short hill. Other bus routes convenient for the Casino Marino are 20A, 20B, 27A, 42 and the 42C.

Temple Bar, Dublin

Lively street markets and alternative boutiques fill the cobbled lanes and alleys of the Temple Bar quarter with life during the day. At night, the area turns into a heaving throng of pleasure seekers flitting from bar to bar, taking in live music, theatre and movies or strengthening themselves at one of Temple Bar's many eateries.

Temple Bar Today

The Temple Bar quarter lies on the southern bank of the River Liffey. The area is roughly shaped like a rectangle and is bordered by the

Liffey to the North, Fishamble Street and Dublin Castle to the West, Dame Street and Lord Edward Street to the South and finally by Trinity College and the Central Bank to the East.

It is hard to believe, but the picturesque charms of Temple Bar could well have been buried under the ugly concrete of a huge bus depot instead. It is a testament to the undefeatable spirit of Dublin folks that the area was rejuvenated, saved from demolition and eventually turned into Ireland's premier cultural quarter.

Temple Bar History

The Vikings settled here in 795. Remains of their settlement's fortifications can still be seen at Dublin Castle. Some 800 years later, the English diplomat and provost of Trinity College, Sir William Temple, had his residence and gardens here in the early 17th century. By the end of the 17th century the area had acquired the name it still goes by today, Temple Bar.

The arrival of a new customs house in 1707 - on the site where U2's Clarence Hotel stands today - brought money and a flurry of activity into the once pastoral area. Warehouses shot up at every corner and taverns, theatres and brothels followed suit.

The boom lasted barely a century. When customs officials moved into new, larger premises on the Northside of the Liffey in 1791, the bubble burst and Temple Bar fell into disrepair.

A run-down inner city slum by the mid-20th century, Temple Bar was long written off when state transport company CIE started buying up property here in the 1980's with the view to building a huge bus depot. While waiting for planning permission by the city, CIE decided to let out the empty premises at cheap rates. Attracted by the bargain rents, artists, fringe boutiques and alternative eateries started to shoot up all over Temple Bar.

The lively, buzzing quarter was received well by Dubliners and resistance against CIE plans to raze Temple Bar grew. Finally, the Irish state got involved in 1991 and set up a non-profit company to oversee the future development of Temple Bar. So instead of buses being washed and serviced on the Southbank of the Liffey, you can still enjoy the unique bohemian atmosphere in Temple Bar's cobbled lanes.

Temple Bar Shopping

Temple Bar's laneways are filled with small boutiques, vintage clothing shops, tattoo studios, record shops, jewellery designers, unusual designer furniture, 60's and 70's retro chic and more. If you are looking for something young and trendy, Temple Bar offers the funky alternative to the more established shops around nearby Grafton Street.

Temple Bar Markets

Street markets play a key part in the Temple Bar experience. The Temple Bar Food Market on Meeting House Square is a Dublin institution. Every Saturday from 10:00 to 16:30, Dubliners flock here to pick up Irish farmhouse cheeses, fresh oysters, local meat products, organic vegetables and handmade chocolates. The Temple Bar Food Market is the place to go for artisanal Irish food products, either as great presents or to furnish a picnic in nearby Phoenix Park or St Stephen's Green.

The Temple Bar Book Market offers a wide choice of secondhand and new books on Temple Bar Square. Practically every interest is catered for, but you will likely find a particularly good range of books on Ireland and Irish topics. The Book Market is on every weekend, Saturdays and Sundays, between 11:00 and 18:00.

The Designer Mart in Cow Lane on the eastern fringes of Temple Bar is the place to browse for handmade clothing and jewellery, arty knick knacks, one-off T-shirts and vintage 70's or 80's fashions. The Designer Mart runs between 10:00 and 17:00 every Saturday from March to December.

Eating Out In Temple Bar

Temple Bar is easily the most 'European' part of Dublin. Whatever the weather, you will find trendy Dublin types sipping their Espresso on the pavement in front of one of the many cafes and snack bars. During the day and at night, life in Temple Bar takes place in the streets - More so than in any other part of town.

If you are looking for a drink or a bite to eat, this is the place to go. The choice is staggering. From relaxed cafes to formal dining, from Italian, Asian, Creole gumbos, Modern European, traditional Irish home cooking to pizza and gourmet burgers - Everything is available in Temple Bar. If you feel like pushing the boat out a bit, the top end choice for formal dining in Temple Bar is the Tea Room at the Clarence Hotel.

For a bit of real Temple Bar people watching, head for the cheap and cheerful Bad Ass Cafe at 9-11 Crown Alley. This place has remained pretty much unchanged since 1983 and is full of typical Temple Bar atmosphere. Ask for a table near the huge glass window front of the Bad Ass and watch the world go by.

Temple Bar At Night

You get excellent pubs and bars all over Dublin, but only in Temple Bar will you be able to literally step out of one pub and straight into the next one without as much as hitting the pavement in between. Temple Bar pubs are always busy and you are almost guaranteed to never have a dull moment.

Music is in the air all over Temple Bar, from traditional Irish folk to the latest international bands and DJs at the Button Factory. If you prefer a quieter form of entertainment, why not join Dublin folks queuing up for a theatre play or a performance at the New Theatre or the Projects

Art Centre. Alternatively, you can watch an Irish made film or an international art house movie at the Irish Film Institute.

How To Get To Temple Bar

The 16, 53 and 123 buses all stop on the southern periphery of Temple Bar. Just ask the driver when you are getting on to let you know when you've reached your stop. The 41 stops at Eden Quay on the northern edge of Temple Bar. The Jervis stop on the Red Luas is a five minute walk away from Temple Bar. Just walk south towards the river Liffey and cross it over one of the two pedestrian bridges: The classic Ha'penny Bridge or the brand new Millennium Bridge

Science Gallery, Dublin

Dublin's newest visitor attraction is the Science Gallery, which opened its doors in February 2008. The gallery offers two floors of interactive exhibitions with changing focus on different areas of science.

Exhibitions typically feature hands on visitor participation and are great fun for kids and adults alike. The Science Gallery makes good use of its extensive floor space, offering many large, walk-through installations which let scientific subjects come to live in a new way.

Science Gallery History

The Science Gallery is the creation of Professor Mike Coey of Trinity College. Coey and his colleagues at Trinity's Centre for Research on Adaptive Nanostructures and Nanodevices (CRANN) launched the gallery on two floors of the Naughton Institute on the edges of Trinity's city centre campus. The exhibition and events programme is the responsibility of CRANN's Dr Diarmuid O'Brien.

Initially, Trinity College expected to attract 50,000 visitors to its newest public attraction in the first year. The Science Gallery proved more popular than expected, with some 120,000 curious sightseers visiting exhibitions on high tech clothing, robots, neuro science and light art.

Science Gallery Events

Upcoming events for 2009 include exhibitions on infections and strategies of containment, the world of extremely small, nanoscale phenomena and a look behind the scenes of virtual worlds based on a virtual model of Dublin.

From April to July 2009, the Science Gallery will show an exhibition and run a series of events under the title Infections. The exhibition will feature epidemic simulations, virus sculptures and more. But it will not all be about gore and grime, as the Science Gallery promises to look at day-to-day phenomena which are based on the theory of infections, such as viral marketing.

Opening Times And Prices

The Science Gallery is open to the public from Tuesday to Sunday. Opening times differ, pending exhibitions. Admission to the Science Gallery is free. Certain events, such as conferences, talks, workshops, movie screenings and others might carry a small charge. Members of the Science Gallery get special discounts on event tickets. You can become a member of the Science Gallery for free by signing up online.

How To Get To The Science Gallery

The Science Gallery is located on the Pearse Street side of the Trinity College campus and can be accessed directly from both the campus and Pearse Street. The most direct public transport link is the Dart, Dublin's light suburban railway line. The Dart stops at Pearse station, which is practically opposite the Naughton Institute building in which the Science Gallery is located. The 128 bus goes from the Connolly stop on the Red Luas line to Nassau Street, a five minute walk away from the Science Gallery. The 92 bus brings you from Heuston station to Trinity College. If you are starting off from the Grafton Street shopping area, Trinity College is less than 10 minutes walk away and it will take you 10 minutes to traverse the campus.

Dublin Writers Museum

Dublin is a city of poets and literature has always played a key role in the city's social and cultural development. You could even argue that literature has been one of the most influential Irish exports abroad. The roll call of Irish writers with close ties to Dublin includes: Jonathan Swift, Bram Stoker, James Joyce, George Bernard Shaw, W.B. Yeats and Brendan Behan to name just a few. The tradition continues with Dublin writers such as Roddy Doyle and Joseph O'Connor penning critically acclaimed, international bestsellers. Discover the roots of Irish literature and delve into the often tumultuous lives of Dublin's famous writers at the Dublin Writers Museum.

Dublin Writers Museum History

The Writers Museum was set up in 1991 to fill a gap in Dublin's cultural scene. The city's rich literary heritage was split into several separate collections and displayed in various locations spread over the city. originally proposed by journalist Maurice Gorham, the Writers Museum was the first attempt to provide a one-stop overview of the most important and groundbreaking developments in Irish writing.

Inside The Dublin Writers Museum

The Dublin Writers Museum is located in a Georgian town house in close proximity to the Hugh Lane Gallery. The museum is compact and aims to give a crash course in Irish literature that will also fascinate visitors who have not been exposed to Irish writers before. Clear and concise wall panels introduce visitors to the main authors and events that shaped Irish literature and led to the creation of still popular masterpieces as different as 'Dracula' and 'Ulysses'.

A personal digital audio tour is available to visitors, filling in the displays with more detail. The audio tour is available in six languages, including English, French, Italian, Spanish, German and Dutch.

Connoisseurs of Irish literature will enjoy the museum's collection of first and early editions of the classics of Irish literature, from Jonathan

Swift's 'Gulliver's Travels' and Bram Stoker's 'Dracula' to Patrick Kavanagh's 'The Great Hunger'. The Writers Museum has also amassed a collection of paraphernalia that once belonged to famous writers, including artefacts like Samuel Beckett's phone and Brendan Behan's union membership card.

Irish Bookshop

The Dublin Writers Museum also houses a bookshop with a choice selection of Irish writers and Irish interest titles. The shop is a great place to browse the works of Dublin's and Ireland's most famous writers and a few more obscure authors. Rather than having to visit several book shops in town to track down what you are looking for, try coming here if you have an interest in Irish history and literature.

Opening Times And Prices

The Dublin Writers Museum is open Mondays to Saturdays from 10:00-17:00 and on Sundays from 11:00-17:00. Admission costs €7.50 for adults and €4.70 for children. The Writers Museum also offers family tickets for €20.00. Events are priced individually. Check the museum's homepage for special promotions.

How To Get To The Dublin Writers Museum

Located at 18 Parnell Square at the Northern end of O'Connell Street, tucked away behind the Rotunda Hospital, the Dublin Writers Museum is only a short walk away from many bus routes. The 3,7,10,11,13,16, 19, 46A and 123 all stop within a five minutes' walk of the museum.

Dublin by Night

Theatres: Ireland is a nation of playwrights and Dublin is the main stage. Some of the more famous names include Samuel Beckett, George Bernard Shaw, Oscar Wilde, Brendan Behan, Sean O'Casey and W.B. Yeats. The tradition continues, and you won't be disappointed if you try a more contemporary Irish play. Theatre is alive and well in venues like The Abbey, The Peacock, The Gaiety, The Gate, Andrews Lane and The Tivoli. Or head for Bewley's Cafe Theatre on Grafton Street for a lunchtime show complete with a steaming bowl of soup and a roll.

Live Music: From international mega stars to underground bands, everybody wants to play Dublin. If an artist tours Europe, you bet they will stop here. Dublin audiences are famous for raising the roof on any of the city's dozen or so music venues. Catch the action at The Button Factory, Crawdaddy, Vicar Street, Whelans, The Village, The Olympia, The Ambassador or at the brand new O2 Dublin.

Irish Traditional Music: Catching some Irish traditional music is a more spontaneous affair. Sessions can spring up in the most unlikely pubs at short notice. Reliable venues are O'Donoghue's (Merrion Row), The Cobblestone (King Street, Smithfields), Oliver St John Gogarty (57/58 Fleet Street, Temple Bar) and in Wexford Street (the pub, not the venue around the corner). If you can't spot any musicians, ask at the bar for the next session.

The Movies: Ireland has a thriving filmmaking scene with Irish-produced movies often turning into mainstream success at cinema box offices all over the country. Some Irish film talent has shot to Hollywood fame, like director Neil Jordan and actor Colin Farrell. A good place to learn more about the Irish movie scene is The Irish Film Institute in Temple Bar, whose book shop and two cinemas are open to the public. www.irishfilm.ie

Dublin Theatre

For a relatively small island at the western fringe of Europe, Ireland has made a disproportionally large contribution to the history of theatre in the Western world. Famous playwrights like Oscar Wilde, George Bernard Shaw and Samuel Beckett are only the tip of the iceberg. Many Irish writers created plays over the last two centuries that are still popular on stages around the world and a new generation of dramatists is keeping the tradition alive. The creative flame is fuelled by lively, passionate audiences.

Dublin has a thriving theatre scene which is typically anything but high brow or overly formal. Dubliners go to the theatre to have a good time. Next time you visit Dublin, why not take in a play and make a night-out of it. Whether your taste leans towards classic or contemporary plays or whether you prefer solid entertainment or biting social or political commentary, Dublin offers a wide range of theatre for all tastes. And don't bother to bring evening wear or a suit

- Dublin's theatre audiences don't go for formalities. Just enjoy yourself.

A Brief History Of Irish Theatre

The history of theatre in Ireland is closely linked to the country's political and economic development. Irish dramatists first rose to wider recognition during the 18th century, a time when Ireland enjoyed economic prosperity and a relatively strong position within the British Isles. Writers like Richard Sheridan and Oliver Goldsmith enjoyed significant commercial success in London. Sheridan was owner of the famous Drury Lane theatre in London until it burned down in 1809.

The golden age of Irish theatre arguably commenced in the second half of the 19th century with Dion Boucicault who achieved great success in New York. Oscar Wilde soon went on to eclipse those who came before him with a series of four plays 'Lady Windermere's Fan' (1892), 'A Woman of No Importance' (1893), 'An Ideal Husband' (1895) and 'The Importance of Being Earnest' (1895). More than a century later, Wilde's plays are still mainstays of theatre companies around the world.

The other figurehead of 19th century Irish theatre is Dublin-born George Bernard Shaw, whose play 'Pygmalion' is a timeless classic. Shaw's play was turned into the movie 'My Fair Lady'.

Coinciding with the strive for an independent Ireland and the eventual achievement of an Irish Republic in the early 20th century, Irish theatre exploded onto the international scene. William Butler (W.B.) Yeats, John Millington Synge, George Moore, and Sean O'Casey are some of the playwrights whose work continues to resound on English language stages.

With independence came a surge in Irish language theatre. The most famous writer working in both Irish and English is Dubliner Brendan Behan. Openly irreverent and sharp-tongued Behan is one of the most celebrated rebels of the Irish theatre scene. His 1950's plays like The Hostage (An Giall) and books like the autobiographical 'Borstal Boy' have aged well and still sound fresh today.

The biggest 20th century icon of Irish theatre is Samuel Beckett, whose 1953 play 'Waiting For Godot' is still synonymous with far out, avantgarde theatre. Beckett won the Nobel Prize in 1969 and his work is still as relevant and moving, more than 40 years later.

A new generation of contemporary writers is carrying the torch of Irish theatre into the 21st century. Marina Carr, Hugh Leonard, Brian Friel and Tom Murphy manage the tightrope walk between achieving critical appreciation and commercial success. Irish theatre continues to travel well, particularly in the English speaking world. Young writers like Mark O'Rowe see their plays performed in New York and many dramatists enjoy crossover success on the television and cinema screens.

The Irish Theatre Institute

If you are curious about theatre in Ireland, then the Irish Theatre Institute offers some useful online resources. The institute offers searchable online databases of Irish plays since 1904, active Irish theatre companies and Irish theatres and suitable venues.

17 Eustace Street, Temple Bar, Dublin 2 www.irishtheatreonline.com

Dublin Theatre Dresscode

The good news is - There is no dresscode to enjoy theatre in Dublin. Dubliners typically treat a visit to the theatre as a good night out rather than a formal occasion. Dress up if you feel like it, but it is by no means required. Smart casual for men and any style of evening wear for the ladies will do. Though you will be just as welcome in jeans and a leather jacket. There used to be a time not so long ago, when trainers or sneakers where simply not done in Dublin, but that has changed and pretty much anything goes in the footwear department.

Dublin Theatre Bars

The place to be during the intervals is the theatre bar. Honour a Dublin tradition and pre-order your drinks at the bar for the next interval. Place your order, pay and return after the next act to see your drinks magically waiting for you in the bar with a little note attached. This system sounds impossible, but it usually works!

Dublin Theatres

Abbey Theatre

The Abbey is the National Theatre of Ireland (Amharclann Náisiúnta na hÉireann) and the first publicly-funded theatre in the English speaking world. Opened in 1904, The Abbey has received a subsidy from the Irish state since 1925. The Abbey has served as an incubator for a large number of Irish dramatists. Famous writers such as William Butler Yeats, Sean O'Casey and John Millington Synge cut their teeth at The Abbey. Balancing the commercial mainstream with the more experimental fringes of contemporary theatre, The Abbey operates a separate, smaller stage within the theatre building, called The Peacock. 26 Lower Abbey Street, Dublin 1: www.abbeytheatre.ie

Andrews Lane Theatre

The Andrews Lane Theatre is tucked away in a back alley between Dame Street and Dublin's main shopping mile, Grafton Street. The slightly grungy outside hides an intimate studio theatre which stages exciting fringe theatre by Irish and international theatre companies. The Andrews Lane Theatre runs regular late club nights at weekends. 12/16 Andrews Lane, Dublin 2

The Ark

Theatre obsessed Dublin has the unique resource of a theatre exclusively dedicated to children. The Ark in Dublin's Temple Bar cultural quarter stages regular plays for children between 3-14 years of age. Many plays shown at The Ark are specially commissioned and have their world premiere at this small but charming theatre in Dublin! 11a Eustace Street, Temple Bar, Dublin 2: www.ark.ie

Gaiety Theatre

The 19th century Gaiety Theatre stages mainly opera and musicals these days. If you catch a dramatic play here, it is typically a hugely popular Irish blockbuster like Brian Friel's 'Dancing At Lughnasa'. At Christmas time, The Gaiety is also home to the traditional Christmas pantomime, or as Dubliners call it: The Panto. This is a real family occasion with children and parents singing along and shouting stage directions. The actual play differs from year to year, but The Panto has been a fixture at The Gaiety for more than a century. The Gaiety turns into a nightclub every Friday and Saturday after the last performance. The disco at The Gaiety enjoys some of the latest opening hours in Dublin. South King Street, Dublin 2: www.gaietytheatre.ie

Gate Theatre

Founded in 1928, The Gate has been instrumental in promoting 'modern' theatre in Dublin. Local son Samuel Beckett featured heavily on The Gate's stage. Famous Hollywood actors Orson Welles and James Mason both started their careers on the stage of The Gate. The Gate Theatre is located at the top end of O'Connell Street, next door to the rock music venue The Ambassador. Cavendish Row, Parnell Square, Dublin 1: www.gate-theatre.ie

Project Arts Centre

The Project Arts Centre has two stages, The Cube and The Space Upstairs. Located in the heart of Dublin's cultural and entertainment quarter, Temple Bar, the Project Arts Centre sets the pace when it comes to contemporary theatre, dance and performance art. Housed in a former printing works, the industrial chic and cutting edge schedule of the Project Arts Centre attracts a trendy, arty crowd. If you are looking for provocative, contemporary theatre, then the Project Arts Centre should be your first stop in Dublin. 39 East Essex Street, Temple Bar, Dublin 2: www.projectartscentre.ie

Tivoli Theatre

The Tivoli Theatre is the new kid on the block, competing head on with the Gaiety, Gate and Abbey. Perched on top of Francis Street with its colourful mix of antique dealers, modern art galleries and old-fashioned Dublin shops and pubs, the Tivoli is a plush mid-size venue that stages mainstream commercial productions as well as comedy and fringe theatre. The Tivoli's 3:00 am licence makes it a popular late night venue, even for people who are not into theatre. Many international top DJs from the Techno and House scenes guest on the decks here.

Francis Street, Dublin 8

www.tivoli.ie

Live Music in Dublin

There is definitely music in the air in Dublin for 365 days a year. Thanks to its young, fun loving population, Dublin is a favourite stop-over for many international superstars and hot, upcoming bands alike. With more than a dozen dedicated live music venues, there is a gig on virtually every night of the week. And that is not even counting in the many pubs, bars and cafes that stage concerts or the open air festivals that take place during the summer. Below you will find a guide to the best music venues in Dublin.

The Academy

The Academy is Dublin's newest concert venue. Set in the former Spirit nightclub, it is a plush, intimate venue that attracts a trendy 30-something crowd. The Academy has a similar L'Acoustics sound rig to the Button Factory. From acoustic gigs to full-on alternative rock, most bands will sound good here. The Academy offers great views from the balcony, which sports its own bar and cosy booths. The Red Luas line stops practically in front of the Academy (Jervis stop). Middle Abbey Street, Dublin 1: www.theacademydublin.com

Ambassador

The Ambassador is the oldest venue in Dublin. Originally built in 1764 as part of the Rotunda Hospital, it was turned into a cinema in 1910. The faded 1950's elegance you can see today stems from the last refurbishment. Today, the Ambassador is a charmingly grungy venue with loads of velvet curtains and red plushy seats. The mid-size venue holds 1,200 and hosts mainly successful alternative rock acts coming into town. Despite the booking policy, concerts here are strictly seated. O'Connell Street, Dublin 1: www.mcd.ie

Button Factory

The Button Factory is a rare thing, indeed - A swish venue with an alternative booking policy. Comfortable sofas and a bar right in view of the stage make this a great place to hang out. The look is minimalist lounge chic and the audience typically young and hip. The sound system by L'Acoustics is out of this world and ranks among the best in Dublin. The Button Factory also regularly books some of the hottest international DJs and the Friday and Saturday club nights at the Button Factory are well worth checking out. Curved Street, Temple Bar, Dublin 2: www.buttonfactory.ie

Crawdaddy

The Crawdaddy, named after the London club where the Rolling Stones made their stage debut, is a small basement venue with a very trendy booking policy. If there is any hot up-and-coming act on the Alternative or Dance scene, chances are they will play their Dublin debut here. The Crawdaddy is part of the POD complex in the disused former Harcourt Street train station. The POD also houses a larger disco and bar upstairs. The Green Luas line stops right outside the entrance to Crawdaddy (Harcourt Street stop).Harcourt Street, Dublin 2: www.crawdaddy.ie

JJ Smyth's

Dublin's only dedicated Jazz venue perches on top of JJ Smyth's pub in Aungier Street. JJ's is all carefully polished 1950's style with a nice, lived-in patina. The pub is a real, no-nonsense Dublin establishment that used to be frequented by Irish author Brendan Behan in the 1940's and 1950's. The literary connections reach even further back: This also happens to be the house that the poet Thomas Moore was born in, back in 1779. The atmospheric venue upstairs books some great Jazz and Blues acts.12 Aungier Street, Dublin 2: www.jjsmyths.com

National Stadium

The National Stadium was built in 1939 as the first purpose-built boxing stadium in the world. The 2,000-seater hall still hosts boxing matches but has branched out into staging mainstream and alternative live music concerts. South Circular Road, Dublin 8: www.nationalstadium.ie

The O2

The O2 is one of Dublin's premier indoor venues. Formerly known as The Point, Dublin's first 'big' music venue, the one-time customs warehouse has been recently refurbished and turned into a high tech concert venue. Big, shiny and clean, the O2 is part of a larger shopping, office and apartment complex. The Red Luas line will eventually be extended to terminate in front of the O2. Until then, your best bet is to walk from the city centre or to take a taxi. Parking is severely restricted while construction work on the rest of the complex continues. If you are a regular visitor to Dublin, you can become a Premium Club Member of the O2 and enjoy fast track access, a private bar and options on tickets for sold out shows, all for €2,500 per year.Northwall Quay, Dublin 1, opposite East Link toll bridge: www.theo2.ie

Olympia

This 19th century theatre turned concert venue attracts many international top acts breezing into Dublin. With its faded elegance and bashed stucco, the Olympia has a charm of its own. There is some standing space on the ground floor in front of the stage. Stalls and Circle are reserved seating and the Upper Circle has unreserved seating. The four bars are a good walk away from the stage, so pick your moment carefully. 72 Dame Street, Dublin 2: www.mcd.ie:

RDS

The Royal Dublin Society (RDS) show grounds are Dublin's premier trade fair and exhibition venue. Due to its size and range of facilities, the RDS is the venue of choice for many international superstars coming to Ireland. The Main Hall has a capacity of 5,000, the Simmonscourt Pavilion seats up to 7,000 and the Stadium can cope with more than 35,000 fans. Ballsbridge, Dublin 4: www.rds.ie

Sugar Club

The Sugar Club is an intimate venue with a carefully studied, old-fashioned night club feel to it. With its Burmese Teak panelled walls and velvet seats, the Sugar Club could have seen Frankie and Dino coming in for a late one in the swinging 1960's. Concerts at the Sugar Club tend to focus on the Funky side, hip Dance acts or happening singer-songwriters. The booking policy is fairly adventurous and stretch into cabaret, burlesque and more. 8 Lower Leeson Street, Dublin 2: www.thesugarclub.com

The Twisted Pepper

Dublin's newest night club, the Twisted Pepper, boasts a mellow vibe and a booking policy that brings the best underground Dance acts from around the world onto its small stage. The Twisted Pepper has space for 350 revellers on its main floor. If the show is any good, the audience will raise the roof at the Twisted Pepper! Concerts here typically start between 23:00 and midnight. Arrive early and you can enjoy a quiet drink at the bar. Middle Abbey Street, Dublin 1: www.bodytonicmusic.com/events/#tp

Vicar Street

Voted best Dublin Venue 2008 and Best Irish Venue 2008 at a recent awards show held by Irish copyrights society IMRO, Vicar Street is a Dublin institution among live music venues. A popular medium-scale venue, it attracts many big name acts, particularly among Irish artists.

The sound can be relatively quiet at Vicar Street and many concerts here are seated. The place is packed with rock memorabilia on the walls and the large bar is popular with a pre-concert crowd. The 123 bus from O'Connell Street or Dame Street stops close by on Thomas Street. 58-59 Thomas Street, Dublin 8: www.vicarstreet.com

The Village

This sleek bar and restaurant sits right at the top of Dublin's newest entertainment mile of Wexford Street/Camden Street. The Village pulls a buzzing crowd into its long minimalist lounge, checking out Dublin's DJ elite on the decks. The Village also hosts concerts in its backroom. If you are coming to see a concert here, please note that the entrance to the backroom is around the back of the block, not through the main bar. 26 Wexford Street, Dublin 2: www.thevillagevenue.com

Whelan's

You are always guaranteed a crowd at this popular bar and concert hall. Whelan's is the quintessential sweaty, heaving rock music venue. It attracts a young crowd from all over Dublin as well as trendy locals from Dublin's newest nightlife strip, Wexford Street/Camden Street. Whelan's has recently been totally refurbished and now features a brand new, decent sound system and good views from almost anywhere in the venue. The balcony has been widened and there's a full bar upstairs now as well. Don't get freaked out by the Stone Man, the life size statue of a lone Dublin drinker which props up the bar to your left just as you come in   He's pretty life-like but definitely harmless. 25 Wexford Street, Dublin 2: www.whelanslive.com

Traditional Irish Music, Dublin

Irish traditional music has been popularised by The Chieftains, The Dubliners and The Pogues. It's no coincidence that all three bands have a reputation as hard playing party animals. Irish music is a soulful, often raucous expression of feelings and a central piece of The Craic, the art of having a good time.

Traditional music is not a stiff, reverential form of art. It is alive and kicking all over Dublin, played by teenagers in hoodies and withered old-timers in suits alike. To really appreciate the music, you have to hear it live in a Dublin pub. Round off your visit to Dublin with a traditional Irish music session for a good time and some unforgettable memories.

The Session

The most likely way you will come across traditional Irish music in Dublin is a pub session. Typically three to five, often more players cram into a corner of the pub and play music throughout the evening. There is no formal programme or set list for a session. The musicians will discuss songs and often one player will suggest a tune and teach it to the others on the spot.

Bear in mind that a session is not a concert. The musicians will only play when they feel like it and the locals in the pub will go about their business as usual. While the pub will fall practically silent during a tune, particularly if well played, the noise goes back up once the song is finished. The breaks between songs can last a good while, with conversations going on and pints being ordered and emptied down thirsty musicians' throats.

Pubs do not typically charge for sessions. But if you like what you hear, follow the local tradition and buy the musicians a round of drinks. There is no obligation, however, and you can just as well enjoy the music without putting your hand in your pocket. Some venues which run a regular session programme or invite big name players may have a cover charge in place.

The session has a special place in the context of traditional Irish music, which developed organically over the centuries. Tunes are seldom written down and largely exist in the heads of the players alone. Tunes then get passed on from one player to the next at sessions. The styles of playing are very personalised and can differ hugely between individuals. Before the arrival of radio and sound recordings, Irish music was very regionalised as players would typically not wander far beyond the borders of their county or even parish so styles would develop in isolation.

That's why a good session is more than a concert. It is a meeting of players where music is created on the spot and - on an exceptionally good night - something new is added to the canon of Irish music for future play.

Traditional Irish Instruments

Traditional Irish music is a largely instrumental affair and vocalists are a rare sighting at sessions. Watch out for a sean-nós session (see below) if you are in the mood to listen to some singing. The instruments used during a session are almost exclusively acoustic. Traditionally, few places would have bothered with microphones and PA systems, so the instruments favoured by session players have a natural ability to cut through the din of a lively pub. You've been warned, so don't stand too close to the potentially ear-piercing tin whistle.

There may the occasional acoustic guitar or even an electric bass, but the mainstay of a traditional Irish music session are the flute and its cheaper cousin, the tin whistle, the fiddle, the uilleann pipes (a style of bagpipe), the bodhran hand drum which looks a bit like an oversized tambourine, the mandolin, the banjo, the accordion and the smaller concertina.

The line-up for a session is pretty loose and you will often find more than one player with the same instrument. They'll either take turns or duet, pending the tune and the mood of the moment. There are some more archaic instruments, like The Bones and The Spoons, which may turn up at a session occasionally.

The Céilí

A céilí is the traditional Irish dance party. This is typically an at least lively and at best fairly raucous affair. A typical céilí band is bigger than the average session group and adds a full drum kit, bass and maybe a piano for a bigger sound that can shake the foundations of a dancehall. The music selection is different to a session, more formalised and with an emphasis on fast dance beats. The backbone of any céilí are the straight four to the floor 4/4 beat of the Reels and the slightly more syncopated 6/8s of the Jigs.

The dancing is typically done in groups, with four couples facing each other in two lines or in a square. This may look like formal set dancing from the outset, but don't worry, the steps are easy and will eventually be ignored by all revellers as the night goes on. The partnering is a pretty light-hearted affair as well and couples exchange partners during the dance.

The most likely way you will come across a céilí in Dublin is as part of a festival or a special event. There are no scheduled, regular céilís in town, as this is more of a country thing. It is definitely worth keeping an eye out for posters or flyers, however, as a good céilí might make your stay in Dublin truly memorable.

Sean-nós: The Blues Of The Irish

The Irish take on the Blues, sean-nós is a dramatic, mournful style of singing. Typically unaccompanied by instruments, a Sean-nós song tells a usually lengthy narrative that can last for five minutes and more. Traditionally the lyrics were in Gaelic, but the style has been adapted to English lyrics as well.

Like the Blues, sean-nós draws its power from blue notes that do not fit regular scales. Sean-nós has many quirks that you won't find in other forms of Western European music. It's scale is modal, closer to a Jazz feeling than what you would typically expect from folk songs.

As with instrumental styles, sean-nós singing differs hugely from one singer to the next. The three main styles of singing you may encounter are the elaborate, ornamental West Coast style, the somewhat plainer Southern Style and the sparse and nasal Northern style.

Traditional Irish Music Pubs

O'Donoghue's

O'Donoghue's pub can be dated back all the way to 1789. The O'Donoghue family acquired the place in 1934 and turned it into a favourite watering hole and concert stage for Dublin's traditional musicians. The pub shot to fame in the 1960s with a new wave of Irish trad bands led by The Dubliners and the Furey Brothers. O'Donoghue's has kept a cool 60's charm, right down to its largely unchanged interior. Sessions here are pretty regular and of high quality. Like all

Dublin pubs, O'Donoghue's is strictly non-smoking inside but offers one of the most picturesque smoking areas in town, tucked away in the old courtyard. 15 Merrion Row, Dublin 2: www.odonoghues.ie/music.htm

The Cobblestone

The Cobblestone on Smithfield is an old fashioned, no frills Dublin pub which hosts nightly sessions by traditional Irish music players. On Saturdays, sessions often start during the daytime and run late into the night. At the back of the pub, the 60-seater Back Room avenue stages regular gigs by artists playing other types of Folk as well as US Country music. Smithfield, Dublin 1

Frank Ryan's

Sessions at this hidden piece of genuine, old style Dublin are not necessarily happening on a regular basis but are pretty brilliant if you catch one. If no session is on, ask at the bar for the next one and order their excellent Guinness while you're at it. Frank Ryan's is located just off Ellis Quay on the Northside of the River Liffey, near the National Museum of Ireland - Decorative Arts & History. If no music is on at Ryan's you can always stroll over to the Cobblestone or cross the road for an altogether different music experience in the trendy and alternative Dice Bar. 5 Queen Street, Dublin 1

Oliver St John Gogarty

The Oliver St John Gogarty is a lively Temple Bar institution that hosts daily trad sessions on the first floor. Sessions typically kick off in the early afternoon and can run until 2:00 at night. There's a separate, smaller Library Bar which often hosts ballad singers. 57/58 Fleet Street, Dublin 2: www.gogartys.ie

Auld Dubliner

The Auld Dubliner on the main Temple Bar thoroughfare hosts daily afternoon sessions from Monday to Friday. At weekends, sessions start at 21:30 and last until 23:30. The Auld Dubliner is not a strict traditional Irish music venue and you may find the odd band belting out Irish drinking songs backed by a keyboard and drum machine instead rather than fiddle and bodhran. 24-25 Temple bar

Whelan's

There has been a pub in this spot since 1772. The present building dates from 1894 and has been a fixture on the Dublin music scene since the 1990s. Whelan's stages rock concerts in a former warehouse at the back of the pub. The list of who plays here reads like an international who-is-who of alternative music. The pub itself stages traditional Irish music sessions and contemporary singer songwriters. Ask at the bar for details of the next session.

25 Wexford Street, Dublin 2

Dublin Cinema

The Irish and particular Dubliners are avid cinema fans. For a relatively small nation, Ireland has contributed a disproportionally large number of directors and actors to modern cinema. Irish movie talent has also made significant inroads in Hollywood in the last twenty years.

Every February, Dublin hosts an International Film Festival which features independent productions from around the globe and the more leftfield output of the major studios. Many successful films had their European premiere at The Dublin International Film Festival, yet it retains a relaxed, easygoing atmosphere. In two words: Typically Dublin.

When you are visiting Dublin, do not miss the opportunity to see the latest Irish movie productions. Below you will find a brief overview of key Irish movies and a list of the main cinemas in Dublin's city centre.

Modern Irish Cinema

Cinema in Ireland had a rocky start. Following Irish independence in 1921, the country was in the grips of catholic values and morals. Irish film censors even cut Hollywood classic Casablanca (1942), omitting all references to Ingrid Bergman's 'Ilsa' character being married as a married woman could not be seen to have a fling with Humphrey Bogart's 'Rick'.

The history of modern Irish cinema begins with a hard kick against catholic repression in Rocky Road to Dublin (1968), a critical documentary of the church and the Irish state at the time. Directed by

Irish journalist Peter Lennon, The film was a hit at the Cannes Film Festival but widely banned in Ireland and only a few daring screenings took place in Dublin during the Sixties. Irish filmmakers had to wait until the more liberal 1980's before Irish cinema would rear its head in earnest.

The First Golden Age of Irish Cinema

Director Neil Jordan rang in the golden age of Irish cinema with 'Angel'(1982). Irish actor Stephen Rea launched his career playing the easy going saxophone player 'Danny', who resorts to murder avenging the death of a mute girl in Jordan's debut film.

'Angel' might have been a slick movie, but it was the love-across-the-barbed-wire drama of 'Cal', Pat O'Connor's movie about the terrorist activities of the Irish Republican Army (IRA) in Northern Ireland, which caught international attention. 'Cal' (1984) was nominated for the Palme D'Or at the prestigious Cannes Film Festival, a first for an Irish film (though, strictly speaking, 'Cal' was an English production with an Irish director at the helm).

Peter Ormerod's absurd portrait of Irish countryside characters in 'Eat The Peach' (1986) and Joe Comerford's road movie 'Reefer and the Model'(1987) have become arthouse cinema classics in the last 20 years.

Irish Cinema's International Breakthrough

The decade was almost over, when Jim Sheridan released 'My Left

Foot' (1989), a film based on the autobiographic novel of Dublin writer Christy Brown. This irreverent tale of the tribulations of Brown and his success against all odds opened doors for Irish film in Hollywood, winning two Oscars. Sheridan followed up his 'My Left Foot' success with the box office smashing terrorist drama 'In the Name of the Father' (1993) with Daniel Day-Lewis and Emma Thompson.

Another director who turned the topic of terrorism in Northern Ireland into a major international blockbuster was Neil Jordan, whose 'The Crying Game' (1992) won an Oscar and grossed $62 million in the US alone. Jordan's gripping tale of a former IRA activist on the run who falls unwittingly for a cross-dressing man who will eventually save him from his former comrades is a bona fide classic. 'The Crying Game' is a cinematic tour de force full of twists and subplots that still work their magic more than 15 years later

The biggest ever smash hit at Irish box offices is still Jordan's 1996 biopic of charismatic Irish freedom fighter turned statesman, Michael Collins. Jordan's 'Michael Collins' manages to show complex historical material with the polish and flow of Hollywood cinema. Hugely controversial at the time, 'Michael Collins' did not shy away from depicting the events leading to the grim Civil War that followed Irish independence.

A hugely influential film in its own right was the English-Irish co-production 'The Commitments' (1991), directed by Alan Parker. The film about a group of youths from Dublin's Northside who launch a Soul band to escape poverty and boredom was based on a best-selling novel by Dublin writer Roddy Doyle. 'The Commitments' brought typical Dublin humour onto the screen in a way that had not been attempted before. Its international success spawned two follow up movies: 'The Snapper' (1993) and 'The Van' (1996). Both based on books by Doyle and directed by Stephen Frears.

Irish Cinema Today

Irish film in the 21st century is taking more of an inward look, with some of the best films focusing on the weird quirks and trials of every-day life. John Crowley's 'Intermission' (2003) starring much in-demand Irish actors Colin Farrell and Colm Meaney is a hilarious take on a botched bank robbery, full of colourful observations of Dublin life.

Paddy Breathnach's 'Man About Dog' (2004) is a laddish comedy based in the circles of the Irish dog racing world. The film was a considerable hit at Irish box offices. Lenny Abrahamson's 'Adam & Paul' (2004) is a dark but sympathetically crafted look at the underbelly of Dublin. 'Adam & Paul' shows a day in the life of two down and out junkies who are falling from one absurd situation into the next. Despite its subject, the film is bursting with real characters and warm humour.

It is interesting to note, that the only major film dealing with Irish history recently was made by an English director. Ken Loach's Civil War drama 'The Wind That Shakes the Barley'(2006) won the Palme d'Or at

Cannes and caused a good deal of controversy when it hit the screens. The majority of Irish cinema goers were deeply moved by the movie and it won the accolade of 'Best Irish Film' at the Irish Film & Television Awards in 2006.

Three Films About Dublin

Sometimes a film really manages to soak up the atmosphere of the location it was shot in. Dublin has been a popular location for Irish and international films alike, but there are three that stand out as a portrait of the city at a particular point in time. 'Educating Rita' (1983) with Michael Caine's sublime portrait of renegade professor 'Frank Bryant' at Trinity College teaching Julie Walters' Northside girl 'Rita' is a good starting point. 'The Commitments' (1991) expresses like no other movie the sheer lust for life of a Dublin on the verge of the Celtic Tiger boom. For a wistful portrait of Dublin at the tail end of the boom, watch 'Adam & Paul' (2003).

Dublin City Centre Cinemas

Cineworld

The largest multiplex cinema in Dublin's city centre boasts 17 screens and shows a wide range of Irish and international films.

Parnell Street, Dublin 1: www.cineworld.ie

Irish Film Institute (IFI)

Founded in 1945, The Irish Film Institute (IFI) is dedicated to the promotion of film culture in Ireland and that of Irish film abroad. The

IFI has a vast archive of Irish film and works to preserve the known body of Irish film productions. The archive's oldest footage dates back to 1897. There are facilities for researchers to view archive footage on the IFI's premises and once a month the IFI picks an archive movie and presents it to the public. The IFI complex at the heart of Dublin's cultural quarter, Temple Bar, houses a two-screen arthouse cinema, a bookshop and a popular bar and restaurant. The IFI shows foreign language films, film classics of the 20th century and independent Irish productions. The programme is eclectic but highly entertaining and the IFI bar is a great spot for a bit of people watching before and after the movie. 6 Eustace Street, Temple Bar, Dublin 2: www.irishfilm.ie

Lighthouse

The Lighthouse is Dublin's newest arthouse cinema. Located in the up and coming Smithfield quarter north of the River Liffey, the Lighthouse champions independent world cinema and offbeat Irish productions. The brand new, high tech building features four screens. Together with the IFI, the Lighthouse has the most adventurous schedule of films in Dublin.Market Square, Smithfield, Dublin 7.: www.lighthousecinema.ie

Savoy

The Savoy is Dublin's oldest working cinema. Built in 1929, the Savoy is full of atmosphere, from the spacious wood-panelled foyer to the upstairs lobby. Following several refurbishments over the years, there is a strong 1960's modernist vibe to the Savoy. Due to cinema's unique character, many film premiere's - particularly those of Irish films - take place at the Savoy.

O'Connell Street, Dublin 1: www.omniplex.ie/cinema/savoy/savoydublin.htm

Screen

The Screen is Dublin's longest running arthouse cinema. The cinema's proximity to Trinity College attracts a young, arty student crowd. There are the obvious Hollywood blockbusters on show here, but the Screen regularly sneaks a good deal of foreign language films and more obscure productions onto its two screens.Hawkins Street, opposite Trinity College, Dublin 2

w

Dublin Shopping

Shopping in Dublin is split between popular UK High Street brands and a multitude of quirky local shops you won't find anywhere else. The High Street brands are generally located on the Northside of the city and the smaller local shops on the Southside. If you are looking for gifts that are typically Irish, head for Nassau Street, which runs right alongside Trinity College. Here you will find a wide selection of woollen knitwear, tweeds, Irish crafts and traditional music in a number of shops sitting literally shoulder to shoulder on the southern side of Nassau Street. Dublin is a very young town with a large number of resident artists, that trend conscious mix is reflected in the small boutiques in the Temple Bar quarter and around Wicklow Street. Dublin is very compact and you can cover a lot of ground in half a day. Do as the locals do, and stop for a coffee or a 'cuppa of tea' and some people watching in one of the many cafes located in between Dublin's shops.

Avoca

The founders of Avoca combined traditional Irish wool weaving with bright, stylish designs in a small village in the Wicklow Mountains. The look fast became fashionable in Ireland and abroad and the Avoca brand has since branched out into ladies clothing, home accessories and more - All in the trademark bohemian, slightly funky Avoca style. The Avoca flagship store in Dublin is a city centre emporium of Irish style spread over four floors. From funky kitchen utensils and delicatessen in the basement, ladies clothing and home wares on the ground floor, gifts and knick knacks on the mezzanine to wooden kids' toys, Avoca is a great store to rummage around in. If you like a sophisticated hippie look with a touch of jet set glamour, this is the place to go, Ladies. Do not miss the opportunity to lunch in Avoca's renowned restaurant on the top floor of the shop. If you like the food, you can take home one of the Avoca cookery books and replicate the experience at home. Suffolk Street, Dublin 2: www.avoca.ie

Grafton Street

Grafton Street is Ireland's premier shopping mile. The wide pedestrian zone invites you to window shop at your leisure, stopping at the many different fashion boutiques, shoe shops, jewellers and the exclusive Brown Thomas department store and its younger BT2 offshoot. Brown Thomas offers the widest selection of luxury designer labels in Dublin while BT2 specialises in upmarket streetwear. The legendary Bewley's Cafe with its picturesque Art Nouveau facade invites you to have a break from all that shopping and enjoy a savoury snack or a cake or pastry from its sumptuous selection on the ground floor.

Georges Street Market

This covered former Victorian market hall with ornate red brick facade and glass roof is home to a funky selection of small stalls and shops. From used books to records, CDs, vintage clothes and streetwear, Georges Street Market is a must for trend conscious shoppers. The market features Dublin's only stall specialising in trendy hats and caps as well as a selection of street food vendors, delicatessen and fine wines. The market runs between Drury Street and South Great Georges Street.

Irish Gifts: Nassau Street

Running parallel to Dublin's famous Trinity College campus, Nassau Street offers great shopping for typically Irish gifts, such as Donegal tweeds, hand knit wool jumpers as well as Irish crafts, traditional Irish music and musical instruments. Within less than a kilometres walk, you can find many local specialities from all over Ireland. At the end of the row of shops, just before Nassau Street turns into Leinster Street South, you find Kilkenny Design, a convenient one-stop shop for typical Irish crafts and fashions of high standards.

Kilkenny Design Centre

The Kilkenny Design Centre is a one-stop shop for established and up-and-coming names in Irish design. In the bright and airy building opposite Trinity College you will find pottery, crystal glass, silverware, wood craft, handmade jewellery, ladies clothes, handbags and accessories by Orla Kiely, Stephen Pierce, Nicholas Mosse, John Rocha and more. The top floor is home to a restaurant and coffee shop overlooking Trinity College. The food and the relaxed atmosphere make this a very popular lunch destination for Dubliners. Nassau Street, Dublin 2: www.kilkennydesign.com

Trendy Boutiques: Wicklow Street

Branching off Grafton Street just in front of the Brown Thomas department store is Wicklow Street, the home of some of Dublin's most cutting edge boutiques and niche shops. Stop for trendy trainers and streetwear at Size?, or browse for fashionable shoes at the Camper and Buffalo stores. You can try on surf wear at Fat Face or get stuck into the vast choice of delicatessen at Fallon & Byrne's - The choice is yours. Stroll down Wicklow Street and turn into any of the small lanes going South - Clarendon Street, South William Street and Drury Street - and you will find more trendy boutiques. If you are looking for alternative music by contemporary Irish bands, visit Road Records in Fade Street off Drury Street, who stock all releases on Irish independent labels.

Funky Streetwear And More: Temple bar

Dublin's cultural quarter Temple Bar is home to an ever growing number of funky boutiques offering the latest in street wear as well as vintage clothing from the 1950's through to the 1980's. From the four floors of Urban Outfitters to small t-shirt shops with exclusive designs, there is a shop in Temple Bar for every taste and budget. Handmade jewellery, tattoo and body piercing parlours as well as contemporary art galleries complete the shopping experience. Pop into one of the trendy music shops like City Discs (Temple Lane South) and Beat Finder Records (Fownes Street) to hear the latest tunes and get tips and tickets for live music gigs and DJ nights in Dublin.

Art And Antiques: Francis Street

Whether you are looking for Irish antiques and bric-a-brac or you are looking to buy some works by Ireland's hottest contemporary artists, Francis Street has the highest density of art galleries and antique dealers in Dublin. Located off the beaten track to the West of Christchurch Cathedral, Francis Street can be reached from Dublin city centre with the 123 bus. Just ask the driver to give you a shout when your stop comes up. Walking down from the northern end of Francis Street, things start off a bit low key with a few old fashioned grocers, pubs and knick knack shops. Halfway down the hill you are suddenly spoilt for choice of classy shops and cutting edge galleries on both sides of the road.

High Street Fashion: Henry Street

Henry Street and its extension Mary Street are a popular shopping destination on Dublin's Northside, running East-to-West between O'Connell Street and Capel Street. On Henry Street and Mary Street you will find many UK High Street retail brands such as Body Shop, Game Stop, HMV, Office, Early Learning Centre and more. Henry Street is also home to Arnott's department store, a Dublin institution, and two sizeable shopping centres, the Ilac and the Jervis Centre. Moore Street, which branches off Henry Street just before the Ilac Centre, is home to a daily fruit and vegetable market. You will also find many ethnic shops here, trading in Asian, African and Middle Eastern groceries and spices. Henry Street, Mary Street and Moore Street, all Dublin 1

Jervis Centre

The Jervis Centre is located directly opposite the Ilac shopping centre and offers a wide range of shops from ladies and men's fashion to books, kids' toys and arts and crafts. Retailers at the Jervis Centre include Wallis, Waterstones and Schuh among others. Henry Street, Dublin 1: www.jervis.ie

Ilac centre

The Ilac centre is home to large flagship stores by fashion retailers H&M and Debenhams. It also features a dozen smaller boutiques plus cafes and Dublin's central public library. Henry Street, Dublin 1: www.ilac.ie

Stephen's Green Centre

Resembling an old time Mississippi river boat with its ornate white metalwork and glass facade, the Stephen's Green Centre features a Benetton flagship store, fashion discounter TK Maxx, a Dunnes department store and several boutiques by surf wear brand Quiksilver and other labels. The centre also features more than a dozen cafes and restaurants, including a TGI Fridays and a Wagamama Japanese noodle bar. King Street South/corner St. Stephen's Green West: www.stephensgreen.com

Designer Shopping: Dundrum Town Centre

The Dundrum Town Centre is Dublin's most upmarket shopping mall with outlets by exclusive London department store Harvey Nichols and a dependence of Brown Thomas' BT2. The centre is home to many UK High Street brands including House Of Fraser, Next, Monsoon, LK Bennett, Molton Brown and more. You also get branches of US brands Urban Outfitters, Timberland and Tommy Hilfiger. The generously proportioned and landscaped centre further features cafes, restaurants and a cinema. The Dundrum Town Centre is located on Dublin's Southside and can be conveniently reached from St. Stephen's Green with the Green Luas tram line (Dundrum stop). Sandyford Road, Dundrum, Dublin 16: www.dundrum.ie

Dublin Nightlife

When it comes to nightlife, few European capitals can offer more choices than Dublin. The city sports a dazzling array of pubs, restaurants, theatres, cinemas, live music venues, traditional Irish music sessions, clubs and late night bars. Dubliners love their craic, the Irish for having a good time. While there may be no 24 hour licensing like in Berlin, locals cram as much fun and excitement into each hour as possible and you will rarely witness a lull in an average Dublin night.

Dublin is a very young and laid back city and this shows in its nightlife. Take it easy and enjoy yourself. Here you find addresses and reviews of the most popular pubs, the happening music venues, the most accomplished traditional music sessions, the best theatres and cinemas, as well as the highest rated and atmospheric restaurants and the trendiest clubs. Dublin is a very compact city and the nightlife tends to concentrate around certain areas. Pick any of the places reviewed here and you will typically find more choices within easy walking distance. Dublin is a fun and comparatively safe city to roam around at night. Start with some of our suggestions and then discover your own favourites.

Dublin Pubs: Dublin pubs are legendary for their unique atmosphere and hospitality. You are never more than a few 100 metres away from a pub in Dublin and there is a pub for every taste, mood or time of day. There is no better place to sample the local speciality, the world famous Guinness.

Live Music In Dublin: Dublin is a favourite stop-over for many international superstars and hot, upcoming bands alike. With more than a dozen dedicated live music venues, there is a gig on virtually every night of the week. If you want some real local flavour, take in a typical session of traditional Irish music in a pub.

Cinema In Dublin: There are five modern multi-screen cinemas in Dublin's city centre. From the gigantic Cine World complex to the ultra stylish Lighthouse Cinema, Dublin cinemas exude their own charm.

Dublin Theatres: Dublin has a thriving theatre scene which is typically anything but high brow or overly formal. Dubliners like both classical and contemporary plays. Next time you visit Dublin, why not take in a play and make a night-out of it.

A Typical Dublin Night: A Dublin night out typically starts with friends meeting in the pub. Then it is on to a restaurant, a show or some live music. Unless there is a night club attached to the theatre or music venue, you'll find yourself back on the street by 23:00. It's still an hour before the late night bars and discos will get lively, so there is time for another round in the pub. Between midnight and 1:00 you show up at the club or late night establishment of your choice to party into the early morning hours. At the end of the night, you stop at a chipper to get a bag of chips, maybe with curry sauce, to strengthen you for the way home.

Relaxed Dress Code: The first thing you will notice about Dublin nightlife is how relaxed everything is. Few places specify a dress code and queues at the door are at best non-existent or at worst fairly short and fast moving. Once inside a venue, you'll typically find a very democratic scene with one bar for all rather than cordoned-off VIP areas, which are a rare sight in Dublin. The locals have a very down to earth attitude towards celebrities, who are more likely to get 'a slagging' or a quick joke directed at them rather than preferential treatment in a club.

Stag Nights and Hen Parties: The relaxed atmosphere and wide choice of nightlife options make Dublin a firm favourite for stag nights and hen parties from Ireland and abroad. Dublin is the perfect city to celebrate that special occasion, be it a romantic anniversary, a family occasion or a birthday party. There is a selection of nightlife activities for almost every taste and budget within Dublin's city centre.

Dublin Events

In Dublin you can find The Craic, Irish for having a good time, any day. Sometimes it is nice to have an occasion, however, and Dubliners have created more than a dozen annual events to have an excuse for a party. From quirky Dublin traditions like the swim in the River Liffey to big, branded events, Dublin has a busy calendar of annual fixtures. In the summer months between May and September, Dubliners and visitors alike are particularly spoiled for choice. Thanks to Dublin's mild winters, the events season lasts well until November.

Dublin International Film Festival: Dublin attracts 40,000 film buffs every February, turning itself into a hotspot of the international cinema. Actors, directors and fans from all over the world gather in Dublin for the two weeks of the festival, attending premieres and viewings of more than a 100 movies. The Jameson Dublin International Film Festival (JDIFF) mixes works by independent film makers from around the globe with releases from the mainstream Hollywood studios for a programme that satisfies arthouse tastes and family demands alike.

St. Patrick's Day Parade And Festival: 16-20th March 2011. New York might have the bigger St. Patrick's Day Parade, but Dublin has turned the one day event into a week-long festival! The city's public places are largely given over to a week of open air events warming Dubliners up for the Big Day, celebrating Ireland's patron saint. The parade on the 17th - St. Patrick's Day - turns the entire city centre into one heaving throng of green-white-and-orange clad revellers. The parade itself is a merry mix of floats, bands and dancers. Only in Dublin could you get a parade that features the mayor's gilded coach followed by Dublin's biker clubs on their Harleys and Goldwings. It attracts an increasing number of dancers, pageants and bands from abroad every year, expect to see groups from the US, Italy and Germany this year. One particularly freezing St Patrick's Day the parade even featured a severely underdressed Samba school from Brazil. That's the spirit! Make sure you wear something green and have the Full Irish breakfast before you go - bacon, sausages, black and white pudding, eggs, mushrooms, beans, the lot. It is a long day and food does not traditionally come into it. You will be thankful for your breakfast later in the afternoon.

www.stpatricksfestival.ie

Heineken Green Energy Festival: Dublin's biggest Rock and Pop festival has been shaking the foundations of Dublin Castle since 1996. Some 50,000 music fans flock to the open air festival which is traditionally held on May Bank Holiday weekend. International headliners this year include Nick Cave & The Bad Seeds, Soulwax and The Kooks. This being Dublin, the festival spills over into various bars in the city centre, with DJs keeping the spirits of the revellers high long after the show is over.

<u>Docklands Maritime Festival</u>: Tall ships line the quays of Dublin on both sides of the River Liffey while traders hawk crafts and exotic snacks on the quays. Street theatre and open air concerts vie for attention with the sailing ships, many of which are open to the public. If the sun shines, seek refuge on deck of a 19th century clipper with a refreshment from the board bar and watch the colourful crowds milling along the quays. This is a busy event, even by Dublin standards - Some 70,000 visitors came to the Maritime Festival last year.

<u>Flora Women's Mini Marathon</u>: 3rd Jun 2011. Dublin's Mini Marathon is one of the World's largest all-women sporting events. It was launched in 1983 and has become a firm institution with some 40,000 runners participating. The 10km course leads through Dublin's green Southside. Just like the full-length Dublin Marathon in October, the Mini Marathon has become a bit of a street party with spectators cheering the participants on.: www.womensminimarathon.ie

<u>Bloomsday</u>: 11- 16th June 2011. A Fancy dress party with a Dublin twist. Fans of Dublin-born author James Joyce dressing up in early 20th century clothes and touring places visited by Joyce's hero Leopold Bloom in the novel 'Ulysses'. In the book, Joyce describes the minute detail of an average day in the life of an average Dubliner. The day is 16th June 1904 and middle-aged advertising salesman Bloom starts frying up his breakfast. Bloomsday appropriately starts with a

big public breakfast fry-up. Needless to say, that a visit to the pub forms part of Bloomsday.: www.jamesjoyce.ie

AIB Street Performance World Championship: 16-19st June 2011: Acrobats, jugglers, buskers and street performers flock to Dublin's green and leafy Merrion Square to battle it out for the title of World Champion Street Performer. The free festival is taking place over four days during which Dublin is turned into the World capital of street performance. Expect contenders for the title to pop up in pedestrian zones and public places across town to practice their skills and build a loyal following.: www.spwc.ie

Dublin Pride Festival: 17-26th June 2011: The Dublin Pride Festival is a week-long celebration of gay culture including sports days and club events. The festival's high point is the traditional Pride Day Parade, which was first established in 2003. This year's parade marks the 30th anniversary of the Stonewall Riots in New York. With an estimated 5,000 participants joining the parade, it is a noisy, colourful street carnival complete with floats and pageants that moves through the city centre.: www.dublinpride.org

Carlsberg Comedy Carnival: July: The Iveagh Gardens
Dubliners like a good joke. They also like to heckle comedians who tell a bad joke. The Carlsberg Comedy Carnival features local and international stand-up comedians working hard in front of a demanding audience. A good spot to see some Irish talent like Des

Bishop, Ardal O'Hanlon, Hector and more. Sneak in, watch and enjoy the banter.

Movies on the Square: July - August

For a few weeks every year, Meeting House Square at the heart of Temple Bar turns into a free open air cinema. If you thought this pub and amusement quarter cannot possibly become any more crowded and buzzing at night, come again. The selection of films is quite wide to suit all tastes, but never boring.

Dublin Horse Show: 3-7th August 2011

One of the main equestrian events globally, the Dublin Horse Show on the grounds of the Royal Dublin Society (RDS) features show jumping and various races with Irish and international entrants competing for big cash prizes and the prestigious Agha Khan Trophy. Horses aside, the show is a well-dressed society event with a party atmosphere. The Ladies make an effort to look glam - There is a €10,000 prize for the best-dressed female visitor. The Gents brush up nicely, too.: www.dublinhorseshow.com

Liffey Swim: 5th September (tbc)

The River Liffey runs through the centre of Dublin. It does not look like an inviting spot for a swim by anybody's standards. But once a year, more than 200 swimmers brave the waters on the first Saturday of September. The race starts at the Civic Offices and finishes at Custom House. The first Liffey Swim took place in 1920. Even though the river is arguably cleaner today than in the 1920, Swimmers still get into the Liffey at high tide; legend has it that there are fewer pollutants in the water then. Thousands line the quays on the day to watch the spectacle and shout encouragement to the swimmers.

All-Ireland Senior Hurling Final: Croke Park

A uniquely Irish sport, Hurling is a bit like playing Hockey without the ball hitting the ground. Two teams of 15 players try to whack a Hockey ball sized leather ball (the Sliothar, pronounce 'slither') with curved wooden sticks (the Hurley) into the opponents' goal. The All-Ireland Final, played at Croke Park Stadium, is the most anticipated game of the year in any Gaelic sport. Dubliners are not big into Hurling, it is more of a country thing and grows in popularity the further South you get in Ireland. Watch the city being taken over by coachloads of mainly rural supporters, 'culchies' in Dublin parlance, who turn all approaches to Croke Park into a street carnival.

Dublin Fringe Festival: 10-25th September 2011

The Fringe Festival offers live music, performance theatre, dance and mixed-media happenings. The festival focuses on artists from around the world who transcend the boundaries between different art forms. The organisers put a lot of quality control into the selection of performers, so the quality is generally quite high and makes The Fringe a great place to discover emerging artists.: www.fringefest.com

<u>Dublin Marathon</u>: 31 October 2011

The 42.2km run through Dublin's Georgian streets is known around the World as 'The Friendly Marathon'. Started 1980, Dublin Marathon is a public street party that attracts 10,000 runners and several times that number in spectators. People lining the streets encourage the runners, crack jokes and generally turn this sporting event into a party.

<u>Temple Bar Chocolate Festival</u>: Dubliners have a notoriously sweet tooth. They also have a soft spot for artisan products. Handmade, speciality chocolates tick both boxes. There is an ever increasing number of local chocolatiers that can fill a square in Temple Bar and hold a dedicated chocolate market to exhibit their sweet temptations. This is heaven on earth for chocoholics.: www.templebar.ie

<u>Christmas in Dublin</u>: During the Christmas season, Dublin takes on extra sparkle, particularly after dark when the city's thousands of Christmas lights are switched on and carol singers line the main shopping streets. Restaurants will be packed with Dubliners getting into the Christmas spirit and Pubs will be roaring with festive cheer, particularly in the city centre. Some cities may go crazy on New Years Eve, but you have to experience Christmas Eve in Dublin. It's the culmination of three weeks of pre-Christmas celebration.

Dublin International Film Festival

For two weeks in February every year, Dublin turns into one of the hotspots of international cinema. The Jameson Dublin International Film Festival (JDIFF) mixes works by independent film makers from around the globe with releases from the mainstream Hollywood studios for a cross section of the most exciting movies of the past twelve months. From intimate documentaries to big drama, the range of films shown during the JDIFF has something for everybody and Dublin becomes a choice destination for film fans every February.

History Of The Dublin Film Festival

The JDIFF was first held in 2003. Over the years it has grown considerably in terms of the number of films shown, the number of visitors and the calibre of actors, directors and other movie professionals it attracts. The festival grew out of the desire to provide a stage for independent movie productions from Ireland and around the world which rarely, if ever, would have found a commercial release in Ireland. In the past few years, the JDIFF makers have successfully integrated more mainstream movies into the festival's programme and the JDIFF has grown from an event for film buffs to a popular Dublin fixture. Many potential box office hits have their Irish premier at the JDIFF and small films which find favour with the festival audience, such as the 2008 Audience Award winner 'Wave Riders', often go on to become surprise box office successes at Irish cinemas thanks to the publicity attached to the festival.

The 2011 Dublin Film Festival

Two weeks, six cinemas, 135 films and 40,000 visitors make the most recent JDIFF the most successful Dublin film festival ever. The previous festivals attracted visits by film personalities such as screenwriter Frederic Raphael, director Hugh Hudson and actors Colin Firth, Clive Owen and Liam Neeson. Thierry Fremaux, Artistic Director of the prestigious Cannes Film Festival in the South of France, attended JDIFF and gave a keynote speech. What started as an intimate underground film festival by Dublin movie enthusiasts has now clearly entered a much larger stage. The Best Film award went to Italian director Paolo Sorrentino for his film 'Il Divo', a portrait of politician Giulio Andreotti who led seven Italian governments in the last 50 years. The winner of the Audience Award was the rock documentary 'The Story Of Anvil' about the heavy metal band of the same name.

Film Festival Ticket Price

A season Pass for the entire JDIFF costs €230.00 and entitles you to attend all screenings and associated events. The Season Pass can be purchased online on the festival's website. Alternatively, you can buy tickets for individual screenings, either directly at the cinema showing the movie or in advance on the festival's web site. Individual film ticket prices range from €9.00 to €15.00 for adults, pending cinema and time of performance. You must be 18 years of age or older to attend screenings and events at the festival.

How To Get To The Festival

Screenings during the JDIFF take place in six cinemas across Dublin. Five of the festival cinemas are located within walking distance of each other in the city centre: The Savoy, CineWorld, The Screen, Lighthouse Cinema and the Irish Film Institute. The sixth cinema, Movies@Dundrum is located at the Dundrum Village Centre and can be reached from the city centre with the Green Luas tram line which departs from St. Stephen's Green.

St Patrick's Day Parade

Ireland celebrates its patron saint St. Patrick on the 17th of March each year. Dublin stages the biggest and most extravagant St. Patrick's Day Parade outside New York. Literally half of Dublin's one million population plus more than a hundred thousand visitors from all over Ireland and from abroad line the parade and turn it into Ireland's largest street carnival.

The Dublin Parade

On St. Patrick's Day Dubliners wear something green, a t-shirt, sweatshirt or even an odd scarf will do, and watch the parade before drowning the shamrock, that is they are having a pint in one of the many pubs lining the route of the parade. More than 675,000 revellers watched the 2009 parade through Dublin's streets. Marching bands from Ireland, Europe and the USA partake in the parade. The music played at the parade ranges from Irish pipe and drum marches to current chart hits and bands compete with each other in costumes and dance routines. The award for Best Marching Band in 2009 went to a German carnival band from the Black Forest. A typical Dublin St. Patrick's Day Parade also features a dozen or more floats and pageants, all extravagantly decorated. Every year, the Dublin parade is traditionally closed by the roar of engines of the city's motor bikers on their Harley Davidsons and Honda Gold Wings.

St. Patrick's Day Festival

Over the years, an ever increasing number of events have been launched to warm up Dubliners and tourists alike for the parade day. Comedy, theatre, music, arts and sports events now form part of the official St. Patrick's Day Festival which lasts for up to a week before the parade takes place on the 17th of March. Many of the events are free and there is a good choice of activities for families with small children.

The Route

The route for the Dublin St. Patrick's Day Parade is 2.5 kilometres long and leads from Parnell Square on the city's Northside down O'Connell Street, over the River Liffey via O'Connell Bridge into Westmoreland Street, past Trinity College at College Green and on to Dame Street. It then turns left at Christchurch Cathedral into Lord Edward Street, Nicholas Street and Patrick Street before finally finishing at St. Patrick's Cathedral.

Times Of The St. Patrick's Day Parade

It is strongly advisable to be at the parade route before 10:00 on the day. The route gets crowded fast and the best spots will be gone well before noon. The Parade starts from the northern edge of Parnell Square, near the Hugh Lane Gallery, at 12:00 noon. It then winds its way slowly down O'Connell Street, past Trinity College at College Green and on to Dame Street before it finishes at St. Patrick's Cathedral. The entire parade lasts approximately two hours. Festivities spill over into Dublin's pubs after the parade has passed. On St. Patrick's Day, Dublin is at its most mellow from 14:00 to 18:00. By then you have seen the best. After 18:00, the locals head for home or their local pub to end the day's festivities on a quiet note.

Grandstand Seat Prices

You can attend the St. Patrick's Day Parade free of charge. However, if you would like to watch the entire parade in comfort, then you should consider a Grandstand seat. Seats on one of the grandstands lining the parade are €60.00 per person. Grandstand seats for the 2010 parade can be bought online on the Dublin St. Patrick's Day Parade's website. Events associated with the St. Patrick's Festival on the day of the parade, such as the Ceili Mor traditional music concert, are typically free. Stalls at the fun fair charge standard prices for rides and amusements. Pubs and restaurants do not typically bump up their prices for the day, but do expect longer queues than usual.

Visiting The Parade With Children

The parade is suitable for children of all ages. Like at all large scale events, parents should be aware that the crowds of visitors make it difficult for kids to see much of the action and that moving through the crowd with small children often requires patience and nerves of steel. You will likely end up carrying your toddler on your shoulders for much of the day.

How To Get To The Parade

Public transport in the city centre on St. Patrick's Day is restricted due to the parade, particularly bus services and the Red Luas tram line. All the main DART stations are operating, however. The closest DART stops to the route of the Dublin St. Patrick's Day Parade are Connolly and Pearse Street. Buses to St. Stephen's Green and the Green Luas tram line are convenient if you want to watch the parade on the second half of its route between College Green and St. Patrick's Cathedral.

Dublin Fringe Festival

Now in its 17th year, the Dublin Fringe Festival presents the best of contemporary avant-garde culture from a variety of disciplines including theatre, dance, street art and more. The festival is much loved by Dubliners and many artists and acts who started at the Fringe Festival went on to become mainstream sensations. Visitors from abroad enjoy the relaxed atmosphere and the world class performances by artists from Ireland and overseas. The Fringe Festival takes place annually in September.

Festival History

Launched in the harsh economic climate of Ireland in the 1980s, the Fringe Festival has grown from an improvised meeting of street performers and small, underground theatre companies into a two week event with more than 100 shows spread across 40 different venues all over Dublin. Despite its size, the Dublin Fringe Festival still champions the unexpected and makes it its mission to stage challenging performances that break with the norm. The Fringe Festival brings the cutting edge of the international avant-garde arts to Dublin and turns the city into a Mecca for art lovers from all over the world.

Dublin Fringe Festival 2011

The 2011 Fringe Festival will take place in Dublin from 10th to 25th September 2011. Last year's theme was a new vision of Dublin shaped by the time we live in, according to the organisers. Works performed during the festival are meant to draw inspiration from the cultural, social and physical landscape of the city. The festival aims high, but entertainment does not take a backseat during the Fringe and the organisers typically select shows that will bring the house down.

Festival Tickets

Some of the performances during the Fringe Festival are free; others require visitors to purchase a ticket. Ticket prices are capped by the organisers with the maximum typically set at €50.00 per ticket. The majority of shows during the festival are priced in the €10-€20 bracket. There are no season passes for the festival as such, but there are 15% discounts for multiple bookings at weekends, the so-called Weekender Tickets.

Getting To The Dublin Fringe Festival

The majority of the venues for the Fringe Festival are located in Dublin's city centre, predominantly on the Southside. Typically, the main venues staging key performances are within walking distance of each other. Part of the Fringe Festival's charm is the mix of permanent venues and temporary open air locations, such as a marquee in a city centre park.

Dublin Marathon

The National Lottery Dublin Marathon is known among athletes as 'the friendly Marathon'. The 42.2km (26.2 miles) race attracts more than 11,000 runners and thousands of spectators line the route to cheer on the athletes from the side of the road or their front gardens. Before and after the race there is plenty of opportunity for overseas visitors to sample The Craic, Irish for having a good time. The organisers put on an Irish breakfast the day before the event and there is an afterparty at the end of the race day for those who can still move a muscle.

Dublin Marathon History

Dublin Marathon is held annually on the last Monday in October, the October Bank Holiday. Instigated by Noel Carroll, the first Dublin Marathon was run in 1980 and won by a two locals: Dick Hooper in 2:16:14 for the men and Carey May for the women with 2:42:11. The marathon is becoming increasingly popular with Irish and International athletes and the field of runners has grown from 2,100 in 1980 to 11,700 in 2008.

Overseas Athletes

Approximately half of the participants in the Dublin Marathon come from abroad. To welcome the international contingent, Dublin Marathon organises a special breakfast run on the Sunday preceding the marathon. Following the run, overseas athletes are treated to an Irish Breakfast and some traditional Irish Music.

The Dublin Marathon Course

The Dublin Marathon starts at Georgian Fitzwilliam Square to the East of St. Stephens Green and finishes in Merrion Square. Both start and finish line are near the city centre. The route passes through Dublin's picturesque Georgian streets dating back to the 17th century. It takes in sights such as Trinity College, Herbert Park, St. Stephens Green and Phoenix Park in a single-lap course. It might be a fairly flat course, but it's not a walk in the park either. The exact route of the Dublin

Marathon changes every year, but runners can expect a few climbs of less than 100m in altitude.

Finishing The Race

Out of the total field, 76% or 9,000 runners crossed the finish line in 2008. This is a notable increase over the first Dublin Marathon in which 67% of athletes reached the finish line. Standards are high, but the Dublin Marathon is still a fun race with many charity teams in the field. Every runner to complete the full Adidas Dublin Marathon will receive a medal, a certificate and a commemorative T-shirt. The overall winner receives the Noel Carroll Memorial Trophy and €15,000 prize money. There is a separate €5,000 prize for the runner who breaks the current track record.

Dublin Marathon Track Record

The current track record for the Dublin Marathon was set by Moses Kangogo Kibet (Kenya) for the men with 2:08:58 and by Tatyana Aryasova (Russia) for the women with 2:26:13.

Recent Dublin Marathon Winners
2010
Men: Moses Kangogo Kibet (Kenya) 02:08:58
Women: Tatyana Aryasova (Russia) 2:26:13
2009
Men: Feyisa Lilesa (Ethiopia) 02:09:12
Women: Kateryna Stetsenko (Ukraine) 2:32:45
2008
Men: Andriy Naumov (Ukraine) 2:11:06
Women: Larisa Zyusko (Russia) 2:29:55

2007
Men: Aleksey Sokolow (Russia) 2:09:07
Women: Alina Iwanowa (Russia) 2:29:20
2006
Men: Aleksey Sokolow (Russia) 2:11:39
Women: Alina Iwanowa (Russia) 2:29:49

Most Recent Irish Winners

The most recent local athletes to win the Dublin Marathon were Teresa Duffy for the women in 1998 and John Treacy for the men in 1993. Teresa finished in 2:39:56 and John completed the race in 2:14:40.

Entering The Dublin Marathon

The Dublin Marathon operates a guaranteed entry system: You pay the entry fee of €70-90 and you're in. You do not require a qualifying time. The deadline for entries for the 2011 Dublin Marathon is 5th October 2011.

Christmas in Dublin

One of the best times to visit Dublin is in December, during the weeks leading up to Christmas. The whole city throws itself into preparations for Christmas Day, but in a typical Dublin twist, the preparations are as much fun as the Big Day itself. During the Christmas season, Dublin takes on extra sparkle, particularly after dark when the city's thousands of Christmas lights are switched on, and the festive atmosphere is simply infectious.

Weather

The weather in the weeks leading up to Christmas is typically mild in Dublin. If November brought a chilly wind, then the temperature rises a few notches in early December. There can be a drizzle in the air, but it will typically be what Dubliners call 'soft' rain. All in all, Christmas weather in Dublin is ideal for shopping and sightseeing.

Shopping

Christmas shopping in Dublin is a feast for the senses. Shops compete for the most striking window displays, carol singers perform Christmas songs and the main shopping thoroughfares are illuminated by elaborate Christmas lights. The Christmas lights in Dublin's city centre are switched on during the last weekend of November. In the weeks running up to Christmas, Dublin's street markets take on a festive atmosphere and you even get a German style Christmas market in the International Financial Services Centre (IFSC).

Christmas Sales

The sales start traditionally on the second day of Christmas, 25th December, with great mark-downs on prices for anything from clothes and jewellery to electronic goods. Particularly the large Dublin department stores like Arnott's and Cleary's typically offer big discounts between the 25th and New Year's Eve on the 31st of December. In recent years, many shops have introduced sales in the week before Christmas. Shop around and you may find some real bargains for last minute Christmas presents.

Nightlife

Christmas in Dublin is the time to meet up with friends you might not have seen in a while. Everybody is getting a bit closer and places to sit and chat in a convivial atmosphere become sought after. Restaurants and pubs are the main places Dubliners celebrate the Christmas season in. If you are planning to eat out it is advisable to book well ahead at this time of the year. Most restaurants will be busy from the first week of December right up to Christmas Eve. Office parties will fill up the tables at lunch and dinner tables in popular restaurants will be desirable like gold dust. Pubs will roaring with festive cheer, particularly in the city centre. Many live music venues in Dublin will have held back the top bands for the busy Christmas season, the average punter in Dublin's clubs and late night bars will be dressed up to party and the city's many theatres put on their most entertaining plays.

Christmas Eve

Christmas Eve is one of the biggest party nights in Dublin's calendar. Some cities may go crazy on New Years Eve, but you have to experience Christmas Eve in Dublin. Traditionally, Christmas Eve is the last hurrah before everybody breaks up and goes home to their respective families for Christmas, it's the culmination of three weeks of pre-Christmas drinks and celebration. The party starts early because pubs and bars will close at midnight. Maybe start with a leisurely lunch. Dublin restaurant staff won't blink an eyelid if you stay for a three or four hour lunch. Dubliners then move on to a nearby pub to meet more friends. They stay here for the rest of the day or move on to the next place to meet up with somebody else. Mobile phones are doing overtime while everybody is trying to arrange to meet up with long lost friends. As a visitor, sit back and enjoy the bustle.

Christmas Day

Christmas Day, the 25th of December, is the one day in the year that literally all of Dublin shuts down. This is the day Dubliners spend with their families or friends, digging into the traditional Christmas meal of turkey and ham. If you are visiting Dublin on Christmas day, the only food and drink you are likely to get is at one of the cities many hotels. If you want to make it festive, book yourself into one of the more upmarket hotels and let yourself be pampered for Christmas.

Stephen's Day

On the second day of Christmas, or Boxing Day in the UK, you go to the horse races in Dublin. The day is called Stephen's Day in Ireland, and only here, and it is a good Dublin tradition to go to the Leopardstown racecourse on the Southside of the city and put a few 'bob' or Euro on a horse. Even if you have never been to the races, the family friendly atmosphere and festive party spirit make this a very enjoyable day out. Leopardstown racecourse can be reached from the city centre by taxi or the Green Luas tram line, which leaves from St. Sephen's Green.

Getting Around Dublin At Christmas

Public transport in Dublin typically runs on normal schedule until lunchtime on Christmas Eve. A special holiday schedule is in place for the time between 24th December and New Year's Day. Please note, that there is no bus, train or Luas on Christmas Day, 25th of December. You will still be able to travel by taxi on Christmas Day. Book well ahead, ideally before lunchtime on Christmas Eve and be prepared to pay more than the regular tariff for your journey.

Dublin Restaurants

Dublin offers visitors a staggering choice of restaurants. The city has increasingly opened up to international cuisines over the past decade and you are now likely to find authentic Chinese food next to regional Italian cooking. The trend among Dubliners eating out has been for Italian, rustic French and Modern Irish cooking over the past few years. But there is a much wider range of flavours and styles to choose from. Eating out in Dublin is a very social affair and restaurants are typically lively any day of the week. Dublin also boasts no less than six Michelin star winning restaurants, four of which are located conveniently in the city centre, among them Ireland's only two Michelin star restaurant, Patrick Guilbaud's.

Dublin Restaurant Prices

Compared to other European capitals, restaurant prices in Dublin are relatively high. Inner city rents and staff costs are steep and give restaurants little option but to pass these on to the customer. Expect to pay €40 and more per person for a two course meal with wine in an average restaurant.

The bill in Dublin's top end restaurants can easily reach €100 per person even without an extravagant choice of wine. If you head for a Michelin star establishment, expect to pay more. Many top class restaurants recently started offering lunch deals as the Irish economy slowed down. If you shop around and you don't mind having your main meal during the day, then there are some real bargains to be had. If you are travelling to Dublin on a budget, please see our suggestions for cheap eats below.

Eating Out In Dublin For €10

The traditional budget meal in Ireland is fish and chips. Fresh fish fillets, usually cod, are coated in a thick batter and deep fried to crispy perfection. The fish is served on a bed of potato chips. In any decent 'chipper' these chips are not French fries, but hand cut chunky wedges of potato. Try some Irish fish specialities like Ray or Rock Salmon for variety. Fish and chips and a cup of tea or a soft drink should keep your meal in Dublin within a €10 budget.

The other restaurant option on a €10 budget per person is going for a Chinese in Dublin's China Town district around Parnell Street. If you stay clear of pricier seafood and stay on tea rather than beer, you can get a tasty and filling meal here for under a tenner. Alternatively, you can head for a Kebab shop. Lamb or chicken from the spit in a pita or flatbread with salad and a soft drink should leave you with change from €10. The Abrakebabra chain has outlets all over Dublin, but for a more authentic flavour try Zeytoon, which has branches in Parliament Street and Lower Camden Street.

Eating Out In Dublin For €20

A restaurant budget of €20 per person will buy you a big slap-up meal plus a few Tsingtao beers in a Chinese restaurant on Parnell Street. Alternatively, €20 brings you within reach of Dublin's many Pizzeria's and Burger joints. Pizza and Burgers do not come cheap in Dublin, watch your side orders and ease up on beer or wine to stay within your budget.

Asian Cuisine In Dublin

If you are in the humour for Asian food but you do not want to limit your choice to one particular cuisine, try Mao. The stylish, modern restaurant on Chatham Row off Grafton Street serves Asian Fusion cooking with a modest price tag and in a lively atmosphere. For Thai cooking, try Diep Le Shaker (55 Pembroke Lane, Dublin 2) or Tiger Becks below the popular Samsara bar (Dawson Street, Dublin 2).

Burgers In Dublin

If you feel hungry for a hamburger in a popular Dublin hangout, try Captain America's on Grafton Street. Rock memorabilia on the walls and groups of boisterous diners give this first floor restaurant its unique atmosphere. Burgers here are usually good, but sides and toppings can be a bit hit and miss. If it's top class burgers you want, head for BoBo Burgers at 22 Wexford Street, right next door to Whelan's pub and live music venue. The beef at BoBo's is organic and the choice of sides and toppings is mouth watering. BoBo is styled like a US diner and has its own bohemian chic. The clientele here is young and trendy.

Chinese Restaurants In Dublin

Dublin's Chinatown is the place to go for authentic Chinese and Korean food. Located on the short stretch of Parnell Street between O'Connell Street and Gardiner Street on Dublin's Northside, you will find a dozen or so Chinese and Chinese/Korean restaurants vying for attention in between Asian grocers and Karaoke bars. Names and menus change frequently here, so stroll along Parnell Street and see which restaurant you like the look of. If a restaurant here looks like it attracts its share of the local Chinese population it must be doing something right. Staff here are usually friendly and eager to help and explain the menu, which may be partially written in Chinese. This is the real deal. Away from Parnell Street, Chinese restaurants in Dublin's main shopping areas or in the suburbs have typically adapted to Irish tastes to the extent that they will likely offer you chips with your main course.

Fish & Chips In Dublin

If you can time your visit to a fish and chips restaurant or 'chipper', then avoid the peak times of 17:00-19:00 (Dubliners getting their 'fish supper' after work) and after the pubs close. When they need to churn out volume, even the best chippers will produce slightly soggy wares rather than crispy goodness. The oldest and best fish and chips shop in Dublin is Leo Burdock's on Werburgh Street, just outside Dublin Castle. Burdock's has the best fish in town - try the huge triangles of Ray - and uses a coal fired deep fat fryer to produce consistent quality fish and chips. Just bear in mind that Burdock's is take away only, there is no seating available. In good weather that's no harm, just eat your meal outside and watch the world go by.

Another option is heading for one of Beshop's many branches across town, which are conveniently located near the main shopping areas and typically offer seating, try Beshop's in Westmoreland Street, for instance. The atmosphere at Beshop's is more akin to a modern fast food restaurant, but the food is usually decent. If you are staying in a

B&B on the outskirts of Dublin, get a recommendation for one of the many local chippers.

Italian Restaurants In Dublin

The Unicorn is a Dublin institution, having served outstanding Italian food in a lively atmosphere for years. The restaurant is located in a picturesque courtyard setting just off Merrion Row at 12b Merrion Court, Dublin 2. If you only fancy a quick bite for lunch, visit the Unicorn sandwich bar and delicatessen on Merrion Row itself. Both the restaurant and the sandwich bar are not cheap, but the food is consistently excellent.

Another top Italian restaurant in Dublin is Dunne & Crescenzi at 14/16 South Frederick Street, Dublin 2. Less pricey than the Unicorn, Dunne & Crescenzi serves up solid Italian home cooking by Roman chef Stefano Crescenzi. Stefano also runs the more upmarket Nonna Valentina in Dublin's picturesque Portobello quarter on the banks of the Grand Canal (2 Portobello Road, Dublin 8). If you are into regional cooking from all over Italy, Nonna Valentina is worth checking out.

If you are looking for Italian food on a budget, visit Dublin's new Italian Quarter on Blooms Lane on the Northside of the River Liffey, opposite the Millennium pedestrian bridge. In the Italian Quarter you will find two restaurants, two Enotecas serving Italian wines and platters of Italian meats and cheeses plus a cafe and a delicatessen. All are very reasonably priced for Dublin and you can dine out here in style for less than €30 per head.

French Cuisine In Dublin

There is many a French restaurant in Dublin but only one as popular and buzzing as L'Gueuleton in Fade Street, Dublin 2. L'Gueuleton serves up plain French Bistro cooking that consistently hits the spot. There is one downside, though: You cannot reserve a table. So come early to avoid the queue. The other place to try for French food is Locks in the Portobello quarter on the banks of the Grand Canal. The chef at Locks is Troy Maguire, who originally cooked at L'Gueuleton. The menu at Locks is rustic French, the setting is atmospheric and it's well worth the trip out to 1 Windsor Terrace, Dublin 8, particularly if you have a romantic dinner in mind.

Michelin Star Restaurants In Dublin

Ireland's only restaurant with two Michelin stars is Patrick Guilbaud's at the Merrion Hotel in Dublin. One Michelin star restaurants in Dublin's city centre are Chapter One, L'Ecrivain and Thornton's. Patrick Guilbaud opened the doors of his restaurant at 21 Upper Merrion Street in 1981. Current chef Guillaume Leburn has consistently kept Guilbaud's at the top of Dublin's restaurant league table. Chapter One at 18/19 Parnell Square would be considered a close second by Dublin foodies. L'Ecrivain at 109 Lower Baggott Street and Thornton's at 128 St. Stephen's Green would come in joint third. All four restaurants are outstanding in their field and well worth a visit for their combination of Michelin star cooking and local Irish produce.

Modern Irish Food In Dublin

The Winding Stair at Ormond Quay Lower is a quaint, bistro style restaurant that has long lead the resurgence of Irish specialities in modern Dublin restaurants. The Winding Stair won a Michelin Bib Gourmande in 2008 and is well worth a visit if you like to sample classy restaurant cooking with a solid Irish twist. Other places to head for a taste of Ireland are the Mermaid Cafe and Cafe Bang. The Mermaid at 69/70 Dame Street combines the cooking of France and New England with Irish flavours. Chef Lorcan Cribben at Cafe Bang at 11 Merrion Row serves up traditional fare like bangers and mash, competently executed with local Hicks sausages.

Pizza In Dublin

Head for the Bad Ass Cafe in Crown Alley, Temple Bar, for good pizzas with a vaguely American touch and some serious people watching. The Bad Ass comes to life at night when the whole hustle and bustle of Temple Bar's nightlife happens right in front of its panoramic windows. The Gotham Cafe at 8 South Anne Street, a side street off Grafton Street, serves good pizzas with a selection of more unusual toppings in a trendy bar atmosphere. Milano on Dawson Street, Dublin 2, is a family friendly place which is modelled on the Pizza Express chain in the UK.

Spanish Cooking In Dublin

There are a couple of tapas bars in Dublin, the place to go if you want somewhere with a buzz is still the Market Bar in Fade Street, Dublin 2. Portions are huge by regular tapas standards and the menu limits itself to a few popular staples which are well executed. Some things here are Spanish by association more than authentic Spanish cuisine, but you cannot fault the lively atmosphere in this huge former market hall which is adjacent to Georges Street Market.

Dublin Hotels

Dublin offers a wide range of hotel accommodation to suit all tastes and budgets. Only in Dublin does The Craic, the good life, not stop at the hotel door - No, The Craic takes place right inside! Hotels in Dublin have played an important part in the city's social life for more than 100 years. Depending on the occasion, Dubliners meet as likely in the hotel as in the pub. Whether it is a family celebration, a cup of tea to take a break from shopping or pre-theatre drinks, if you grew up in Dublin you will head for one of the city's hotels. And don't forget that the residents bars of Dublin's hotels are most likely the last place in town where you can get a drink after a night's celebrations.

Bewleys Ballsbridge Hotel: The Bewleys group runs two hotels in Dublin, one in the southern suburb of Leopardstown - near Dublin's horse racing course - and one closer to the city centre in leafy and exclusive Ballsbridge. The Ballsbridge Bewleys is located directly opposite the Four Seasons luxury hotel and close to the show grounds of the Royal Dublin Society, the RDS. Bewleys Hotel Ballsbridge takes up the spectacular red brick architectur of a former 19th century Masonic School. If you are travelling on a budget it is worth checking out Bewleys Ballsbridge as the hotel consistently offers some of the keenest room rates and family deals on Dublin's Southside.: www.bewleyshotels.com

The Burlington: Known among Dubliners simply as 'the Burlo', the Burlington has been at the hub of Dublin society since it opened its doors in 1972. Located on Upper Leeson Street in exclusive Dublin 4, the Burlington's ballroom is the spot for major black tie and little black dress get togethers from awards shows, masked balls and sports galas to charity events.: www.burlingtonhotel.ie

The Clarion: The Clarion Hotel lies in the middle of Dublin's financial district, the International Financial Services Centre or IFSC. The hotel is overlooking the River Liffey and has its own fitness centre complete with 18 metre indoor pool. If you are visiting Dublin during the annual Maritime Festival, then a stay at the Clarion Hotel will put you right in the thick of the action. The Clarion is also the nearest hotel to Dublin's largest purpose-built concert venue, the O2. The hotel is a 10 minute walk away from Connolly train station and the Red Luas tram line. The Luas rail system is currently being extended along the quays and will connect the Clarion with the O2 concert venue.: www.clarionhotelifsc.com

Clontarf Castle: The Clontarf Castle Hotel stands on historic grounds. It was here that Irish chieftain Brian Boru gave the Vikings one of their rare defeats. These days, Clontarf is a quiet, elegant seaside town full of Victorian red brick houses just to the north of Dublin's city centre. The earliest parts of Clontarf Castle date back to 1172. The main building was re-built in 1837. The castle is hidden away from the town on its own, secluded grounds and housed a cabaret for 25 years before it became a hotel in 1998. The ivy-clad exterior of Clontarf Castle houses a modern hotel that incorporates many antiques from the castle's history. There is a definite Tudor touch about the lobby and some of the main public rooms with their flagstone floors, stone walls and dark wooden beams. Clontarf Castle is located close to Eastpoint Business Park and convenient for Dublin Airport and Dublin Port.: www.clontarfcastle.ie

The Conrad: The Conrad is a modern five-star hotel located on quiet Earlsfort Terrace, just off St. Stephen's Green. Rooms at The Conrad are overlooking the National Concert Hall. The hotel is a short stroll from a secluded gem of a park, Iveagh Gardens. If you are planning to visit Dublin on St. Patricks Day, the Irish national holiday on the 17th of March, then The Conrad lies at the heart of the action. The St. Patricks Day Festival concert stage which hosts the Ceili Mor (Irish for

'Big Party') is traditionally located on Earlsfort Terrace within view - and earshot - of the hotel.: http://conradhotels1.hilton.com

The Fitzwilliam Hotel : The Fitzwilliam hotel is located directly on St. Stephen's Green at the heart of Dublin. A two-minute stroll from Dublin's main shopping mile, pedestrianised Grafton Street, the Fitzwilliam is a popular meeting spot with its three restaurants, which include the Michelin star bearing Thorntons. Under the direction of chef Kevin Thornton, the restaurant is a favourite with Dublin foodies.: www.fitzwilliamhotel.com

The Gresham: Founded in 1817, The Gresham is a Dublin institution on O'Connell Street. The only four star hotel on Dublins main north-south thoroughfare, The Gresham is a popular spot for lunch or afternoon tea. The hotel lies across the road from the General Post Office, the setting for the Easter Rising of 1916, an important milestone on the way to Irish independence. The Gresham Hotel is also very convenient for the Hugh Lane Gallery and the most popular shopping area on Dublin's Northside, Henry Street.: www.gresham-hotels.com

Herbert Park Hotel: You get to feel like a well heeled Dubliner turning into the leafy residential road that leads to the Herbert Park Hotel. The hotel sits in a modern apartment complex among posh red brick terraces a few minutes' walk away from the grounds of the Royal Dublin Society, the RDS. Rooms at the Herbert Park Hotel overlook the

48 acre park of the same name. The park has a genteel, old-fashioned feel, complete with a bowling green and a duck pond.: www.herbertparkhotel.ie

Jurys Inn Christchurch: The Jurys Inns group has three hotels in Dublin: Custom House, Parnell Street and Christchurch. Jurys Inn Christchurch is the most convenient for sightseeing, situated right opposite Christchurch Cathedral and Dublinia and a short walk from Dublin Castle, St. Patrick's Cathedral, and the Guinness Storehouse.: http://dublinhotels.jurysinns.com/

The Morgan: The Morgan on the fringes of Dublin's Temple Bar area packs a young, fashionable crowd into its bar. One of the most cutting edge venues in Temple Bar, The Morgan even has its own series of chill-out music compilation CDs. Upstairs from the stylish bar you will find equally cool living quarters. The Morgan's most spectacular room is the Penthouse, which gives you a unique view over the roofs of Dublin. The Penthouse at the Morgan has furniture by French designer Philippe Starck and you can entretain up to 35 guests up here.: www.themorgan.com

The Morrison: Situated right on the quays overlooking the River Liffey, the Morrison is the only boutique hotel on Dublin's Northside. The cool grey glass facade of the Morrison's ground floor bar is a landmark on the quays. A trendy young crowd gathers here in the Morrison Hotel's stark, minimalist chic. Originally designed by Irish fashion and interior design icon John Rocha, the Morrison does not only look good, it is comfortable too.: www.morrisonhotel.ie

O'Callaghan Stephen's Green: The O'Callaghan group owns four hotels in Dublin: The Davenport, the Alexander, the Montclair and the O'Callaghan Stephen's Green. All hotels have four stars bar the three star Montclair. The Alexander, Davenport and Montclair are located within view of each other in a side street just off Merrion Square with its magnificient Georgian townhouses. The Stephen's green hotel is the most convenient for shopping, thanks to its location near St. Stephen's Green and the southern end of Grafton Street.: www.ocallaghanhotels.com

The Westbury: Tucked away in a quiet location just off Dublin's main shopping mile, Grafton Street, The Westbury is a Dublin institution for family lunches and get-togethers. The hotel is a haven for shopaholics, situated close to Grafton Streets fashionable boutiques and boasts its own, exclusive Westbury Shopping Mall with an eclectic mix of shops from jewellers to top end kids fashions. The Westbury has recently been refurbished and now offers amenities such as complimentary high speed internet access, 32" flat screen TVs and iPod docking stations in its rooms.: www.doylecollection.com

The Westin : The Westin Hotel overlooks Trinity College and the historic Bank Of Ireland building which housed the Irish Parliament during the 18th century. The Westin is located in the opulent former headquarters of Allied Irish Bank just off College Green. The Temple Bar area starts literally on the opposite side of the road from the Hotel's main entrance. The northern end of Dublin's main shopping mile, Grafton Street, lies a five-minute stroll away.: www.thewestindublin.com

Bewleys Ballsbridge Hotel

Bewleys Ballsbridge Hotel is equally suited to families on vacation in Dublin and business travellers attending an exhibition at the nearby RDS. Public rooms and bedrooms are furnished in a modern, neutral colour scheme.

Location: Bewleys Ballsbridge Hotel is located in Dublin's embassy quarter, close to the show grounds of the Royal Dublin Society, the RDS. The hotel takes up the spectacular red brick architecture of a former 19th century Masonic School, set back from the main road in its own, landscaped grounds.

Room Rates: The hotel offers double, twin and spacious family rooms. Doubles start at €59.00 per room per night, which is outstanding value for the area close to the city centre. A full Irish breakfast is available at the price of €12.00 per person, which will be added to your bill. There are smoking and non-smoking rooms available. Family rooms accommodate two adults and up to three children under 16.

Facilities: Bewleys Ballsbridge Hotel offers free wireless broadband internet access in all bedrooms and throughout the building. Please note that some bedrooms have WiFi access only. The hotel has a stylish restaurant, which wraps around a stunning atrium and offers local Irish produce and specialities. A special children's menu is available.

Meeting & Function Rooms: The hotel has meeting and conference rooms for 12 to 200 delegates. Room hire is available from as little as €175.00 per day and includes technical equipment such as projectors, screens, flip charts and direct dial phone. The Bewleys Ballsbridge conference facilities are very convenient if you want to schedule a private meeting to coincide with an industry trade fair or other event at the RDS.

How To Get To Bewleys Ballsbridge Hotel: Bewleys Ballsbridge is located at the corner of Merrion Road and Simmonscourt Road. A taxi from Dublin Airport will take approximately 40 minutes and cost €30.00. Alternatively, you can take the Aircoach bus service to and from the airport, which stops directly in front of the hotel. The nearest DART station is Sandymount. Bus routes 7 and 45 stop on Merrion Road close to the hotel. The hotel has a large underground car park. Parking is available at the price of €8.00 per day for hotel guests.

Phone: + 353 (0)1 668 1111
Fax: + 353 (0)1 668 1999
E-mail: Ballsbridge@BewleysHotels.com

The Burlington Hotel

The Burlington Hotel offers 500 bedrooms and conference facilities for up to 1,300 delegates in close proximity to the city centre. The Burlo, as it is known among Dubliners, is the venue of choice for gala events in central Dublin and offers stylish accommodation.

Location: The Burlington is located on Upper Leeson Street, just South of the picturesque Grand Canal. You can walk from the hotel to St. Stephen's Green in 15 minutes. The Burlington is very convenient for offices located in the South inner city between Grand Canal Dock and Harcourt Street.

Room Rates At The Burlington: Standard doubles start at €109.00 per room per night, excluding breakfast. Executive rooms are available from €129.00 per room per night. Executive room rates include free continental breakfast, express checkout and access to the executive gym and lounge. The Burlington offers discounts up to 40% for long term stays and often has special offers for last minute bookings.

Meeting & Function Rooms: The Burlington hotel offers 18 meeting rooms for groups of 5 to 800 delegates. Room configuration and seating are very flexible and allow you to tailor the size to the type of event you are planning and the number of attendants you are expecting. The Burlington's elegant Ballroom can accommodate up to 1,200 guests. You can also hire the hotel's entire ground floor, which will provide ample space for 1,300 delegates. Room hire starts at

€550.00 per day. The Ballroom is available for €10,000 per day. Other rates available on request.

Facilities: All bedrooms have complimentary high speed Internet access. Free WiFi Internet access is available throughout the public rooms and all conference facilities. The Burlington further offers executive guests a private 6th floor lounge with views over Dublin's South inner city and a gym, also located on the 6th floor. The Burlington features two restaurants and two separate bars. The resident's bar at the Burlington stays open until 2:00.

How To Get To The Burlington: Travelling from Dublin Airport, a taxi ride will take approximately 45 minutes, pending traffic, and cost €30.00. The Aircoach bus service to and from Dublin Airport stops across the road from the Burlington on the corner of Upper Leeson Street and Appian Way. A single journey on the Aircoach costs €8.00. A taxi to and from a city centre location will cost approximately €8.00 to €12.00. Bus routes 11/11A and 46/46A to Stillorgan stop close to the Burlington.

Phone : +353 (0)1 618 5600
Fax : +353 (0)1 668 8086
E-mail : info@burlingtonhotel.ie

The Clarion Hotel

The Clarion is a modern hotel with minimalist chic offering family and business accommodation at the heart of Dublin's financial district. The hotel is overlooking the River Liffey and has its own fitness centre with 18 metre indoor pool and a spa offering massages and health treatments.

Location: The Clarion is located on Custom House Quay in the middle of Dublin's financial district, the International Financial Services Centre, overlooking the River Liffey. The Clarion is the closest hotel to Dublin's premier concert venue, the O2, which lies a short 10 minute walk down the quays.

Room Rates: Standard queen size bed doubles start from €99.00 per room per night, excluding breakfast. The Clarion spends great care on detail, such as Egyptian cotton bed linen and quality toiletries in all rooms. Suites start from €174.00 per night when booked online. Please specify the Clarion's Internet Saver rate when booking.

Meeting & Function Rooms: The Clarion has eight modern and well equipped meeting rooms overlooking Dublin's booming Docklands and the River Liffey. Rooms are available for parties from 10 to 110 delegates. Room configuration and seating can be adapted to the style of your meeting and the number of attendants. Meeting room hire starts at €200.00 per day. The Clarion also offers full delegate packages including room hire, light lunch, pastries, tea and coffee from €55.00 per delegate.

Facilities: The Clarion features a Sanovitae health and fitness club with full spa treatment facilities, an 18 metre swimming pool as well as a sauna, steam room and Jacuzzi. The hotel offers a babysitting service for parents travelling with small children. Complimentary broadband Internet access is available in all bedrooms. Sony Playstation and Nintendo Wii gaming consoles are available on request. The Kudos restaurant at the Clarion offers Asian fusion cooking in a modern, relaxed atmosphere.

How To Get To The Clarion: Its location close to Dublin port and the Port Tunnel makes the Clarion very convenient for Dublin airport. A taxi ride from or to the airport should take less than 30 minutes, pending traffic, and cost approximately €20.00 to €25.00. The hotel is a 10-minute walk away from Connolly train station, which is serviced by the DART, all major suburban rail services and the main Dublin to Belfast line. The Red Luas tram line also stops at Connolly. The Luas is currently being extended along the quays and will eventually stop nearer to the hotel.

Phone : +353 (0)1 4338800
Fax : +353 (0)1 4338811
E-mail : info@clarionhotelifsc.com

Clontarf Castle Hotel Dublin

Voted Business Hotel of The Year 2008 by Georgina Campbell's Ireland Guide, the Clontarf Castle hotel offers flexible conference facilities and easy access to the main office parks and industrial estates on Dublin's Northside. Located in an ivy-clad former castle, the style of the hotel's public areas and bedrooms are quaintly old-fashioned rather than modern and incorporate many Tudor touches.

Clontarf Castle History: Irish chieftain Brian Boru gave the Vikings one of their rare defeats at the former port of Clontarf in 1014. The earliest parts of Clontarf Castle date back to 1172. The main building was re-built in 1837. The castle is hidden away from the town on its own, secluded grounds and housed a cabaret for 25 years before it became a hotel in 1998.

Location: Clontarf Castle is located in the quiet, elegant seaside town of Clontarf, just to the north of Dublin's city centre.

Room Rate: Deluxe doubles at Clontarf Castle start from €93.00 per room per night, excluding breakfast. Bed and full Irish breakfast for two starts from €118.00 per night. All bedrooms have broadband Internet access and feature European as well as US AC sockets. For a supplement, you can upgrade to an Executive room with a four poster bed. Executive upgrades are available from €60.00 per room per night.

Meeting & Function Rooms: Clontarf Castle offers four conference rooms for 10 to 200 delegates. In addition to the dedicated meeting rooms, the castle's Great Hall can accommodate up to 600 guests. Clontarf Castle offers a conference package including room hire, light lunch, tea and coffee from €50.00 per delegate per day.

Facilities: Clontarf Castle has a small gym on the lower ground floor. If you would like to use more extensive fitness facilities, the hotel will arrange a special discount with the nearby Westwood health club, which offers a full size gym, tennis, squash and a 50m indoor pool. For business travellers, the hotel operates a courtesy coach to nearby Eastpoint Business Park from Monday to Friday.

How To Get To Clontarf Castle: Clontarf Castle is located off Castle Avenue in Clontarf, Dublin 3. A taxi ride from or to Dublin airport will take about 30 minutes, pending traffic and set you back approximately €20.00. The most convenient DART station is Clontarf Road. Upon leaving the station, take the 130 bus from Clontarf Road which will drop you off in front of the castle grounds

Phone: + 353 (0)1 8332321
Fax: + 353 (0)1 8330418
E-Mail: info@clontarfcastle.ie

Conrad Hotel Dublin

The Conrad is a five-star hotel which is part of the international Hilton group of hotels. Bright, modern bedrooms and a quiet but convenient city centre location make the Conrad ideal for business and leisure. The Conrad's stylish lobby is a popular destination with Dubliners for a leisurely afternoon tea.

Location: The Conrad Hotel Dublin is located conveniently in a quiet side street just off St. Stephen's Green. Some of the bedrooms are

165

overlooking Rooms the National Concert Hall and secluded Iveagh Gardens. The Conrad is within easy walking distance of many popular restaurants and Dublin's exciting nightlife.

Room Rates At The Conrad: A Classic King Size double bedroom with king size bed starts from €178.00 per room per night, excluding breakfast. The Conrad offers a special bed and breakfast rate from €202.00 for two persons per night. Junior Suites with a separate sitting room start from €234.00 and Business Suites from €319.00 per night for the room only, or €262.00/€352.00 including breakfast.

Meeting & Function Rooms: The Conrad offers 12 meeting rooms for events, from the Boardroom for 12 executives to the Ballroom for up to 350 guests. Please contact the hotel directly for a quote.

Facilities: All bedrooms have high speed Internet access and feature 25inch flat screen TVs and a HiFi system with CD player. Guests are provided with bathrobes and slippers for the duration of their stay. The Alex restaurant at the Conrad offers a good selection of seafood dishes and local produce, often sourced from organic farms. The Conrad Hotel also provides 24-hour room service. A fitness centre and gym is available for the exclusive use of hotel guests.

How To Get To The Conrad Dublin: A taxi from or to Dublin airport will take 40 minutes, pending traffic and the fare will amount to approximately €30.00. Both the St. Stephen's Green and Harcourt stops on the Green Luas tram line can be reached from the Conrad within a short walk. The nearest DART station is Pearse Street, which is a brisk 15 minute walk away from the hotel, past St. Stephen's Green and leafy Merrion Square.

Phone: +353 (0)1 602 8900
Fax (Reservations): +353 (0)1 676 5424
E-mail: dublininfo@conradhotels.com

Fitzwilliam Hotel Dublin

The Fitzwilliam has been styled by interior design guru Sir Terence Conran from the furniture right down to the bedlinen. Enjoy five star luxury with a truly modern touch at this city centre hotel. The Fitzwilliam is home to one of Dublin's Michelin star restaurants, the celebrated Thorntons.

Location: The Fitzwilliam designer hotel is located on St. Stephen's Green park, the green heart of Dublin. The hotel is only a two-minute stroll from Dublin's main shopping mile Grafton Street.

Room Rates At The Fitzwilliam Hotel: The Fitzwilliam is a designer hotel through and through. From Egyptian linen and luxury bathrobes to 28" LCD TVs, all rooms are decorated and fitted out to high standards. Doubles start from €160.00 per room per night excluding breakfast. Bed and breakfast packages start from €195.00 per night for two persons. Suites start from €275.00 per room per night. The Penthouse Suite at the Fitzwilliam comes with its own private bar and butler and costs €3,200.00 per night.

Meeting And Function Rooms: The Fitzwilliam has three meeting rooms which can cater for 16 up to 100 delegates. All three rooms are equipped for video conferencing and offer complimentary wireless and wired broadband Internet access. Meeting room hire starts from €500.00 per day. PA system and other equipment are charged extra.

Facilities: All bedrooms come with complimentary broadband Internet access, mineral waters and newspapers. The Fitzwilliam offers 24-hour room service, a fitness suite, a hair and beauty salon as well as same day laundry service. The hotel has two restaurants, the informal Citron and the Michelin star winning Thorntons.

How To Get To The Fitzwilliam Hotel: The most direct way to reach the Fitzwilliam Dublin Hotel from Dublin airport is by taxi. The journey will take approximately 40 minutes, pending traffic. Be prepared to pay €25.00-€30.00 for a single trip. The Green Luas tram line is convenient for journeys on Dublin's Southside. The Green Luas terminus at St. Stephen's Green is located practically in front of the hotel. A large number of bus routes pass College Green at the top end of Grafton Street, a 10-minute stroll away.

Phone : +353 (0)1 478 7000
Fax : +353 (0)1 478 7878
E-mail : enq@fitzwilliamhotel.com

Gresham Hotel Dublin

The four star Gresham Hotel has been refurbished in 2006 and offers comfortable accommodation in timeless style. The hotel dates back to 1817 and its individual quirks mean that every room here is slightly different. Ask to see a few rooms to judge layout, decor and view.

Location: The hotel is situated on O'Connell Street opposite the General Post Office, the setting for the Easter Rising of 1916, an important milestone on the way to Irish independence. The Gresham Hotel is located very conveniently for the Hugh Lane Gallery, the Dublin Writers Museum and the most popular shopping area on Dublin's Northside, Henry Street.

Room Rates At The Gresham: Standard doubles at the Gresham start from €99.00 per room per night, excluding breakfast. Bed and breakfast for two starts from €135.00 per night. To upgrade to a queen size bed or a room overlooking O'Connell Street, you will need to pay a supplement of €60.00 per room per night. Penthouse suites overlooking Dublin's skyline start from €2,000.00 per night.

Meeting And Function Rooms: The Gresham features 20 meeting rooms spread over four floors which can cater for groups from 16 to 350 delegates. Half day rates start from €280.00 and full day room hire starts from €420.00. PA system and other audiovisual equipment are charged extra. Full conference catering is available from €16.00 per person.

Facilities: All bedrooms come with complimentary wired and WiFi Internet access. The Gresham offers 24-hour room service. A babysitting service is available on request for parents travelling with small children. The hotel has an air-conditioned gym with complimentary mineral water and towels for guests. The Writer's Bar with its old world charm, dim lighting and comfortable couches is a traditional tea time location for Dubliners. A good old fashioned Tea is served from 14:00 to 18:00 and costs €25.00 per person.

How To Get To The Gresham: The Gresham is conveniently located for Dublin airport, Connolly train station and the ferry terminal at Dublin Port. A taxi ride from or to the airport will take approximately 30 minutes, pending traffic and cost about €25.00. The Aircoach bus service to and from Dublin airport stops right in front of the Gresham Hotel. A single fare on the Aircoach from the airport to the Gresham costs €7.00. O'Connell Street is serviced by a large number of bus routes. The Red Luas tram line stops in Abbey Street, a five minutes' walk from the hotel.

Phone: +353 (0)1 874 6881
Fax: +353 (0)1 878 7175
E-mail: info@thegresham.com

Herbert Park Hotel Dublin

The Herbert Park Hotel offers sleek, modern style in a quiet park setting. This contemporary urban retreat is nevertheless only a stone's throw away from Dublin's main exhibition grounds, the RDS, and a short taxi ride from the city centre.

Location: The main entrance to the Herbert Park Hotel is located on Anglesea Road, opposite the Royal Dublin Society (RDS) exhibition complex. The Herbert Park Hotel lies at the heart of leafy Ballsbridge, Dublin's most exclusive residential address. The hotel itself stretches along the edges of Herbert Park, a green 48 acre oasis amidst the embassies and villas of Ballsbridge.

Room Rates At The Herbert Park Hotel: Single rooms start from 99.00 excluding breakfast. Standard doubles are available from €109.00 with special bed and breakfast deals starting from €129.00 for two mid-week. Executive rooms all feature Jacuzzi baths and start from €159.00 per room per night. Penthouse Suites come equipped with Bang & Olufsen HiFi and TV as well as a private balcony offering great views over Dublin. Suites start from €550.00 per night.

Meeting And Function Rooms: The Herbert Park Hotel has eight meeting rooms which can accommodate between 2 and 250 delegates. Many of the hotels meeting rooms benefit from natural daylight. The audio visual equipment includes WiFi , ceiling mounted data projectors, drop down screens and integrated PA systems.

Facilities: The hotel's Terrace Lounge and Pavilion restaurant invite you to relax and enjoy the tranquil setting on the edge of Herbert

Park. The Herbert Park Hotel offers 24-hour room service, a private fitness suite for guests and secure underground parking.

How To Get To The Herbert Park Hotel: A taxi from or to Dublin airport will take about 45 minutes and cost approximately €30.00. The Aircoach to and from Dublin airport stops on Merrion Road at the top of Anglesea Road, a few minutes' walk from the main entrance to the Herbert Park Hotel. A single ticket on the Aircoach between Dublin airport and the Herbert Park Hotel is €8.00. The nearest DART station is a 10 minute walk away at Lansdowne Road. Upon leaving the station, turn right and walk up Lansdowne Road until you reach the traffic lights. Turn into Shelbourne Road and follow until you come to the main junction and you see the RDS in front of you. Cross the main road, and keep on straight ahead, you are now on Anglesea Road and the hotel is immediately to your right once you are going past the gates for the RDS.

Phone: + 353 (0)1 667 2200
Fax: +353 (0)1 667 2595
Email: reservations@herbertparkhotel.ie

Jurys Inn Christchurch Dublin

Jurys Inn Christchurch enjoys a fantastic location from a tourist's point of view, bringing at least half of Dublin's attractions within easy reach. Accommodation at Jurys Inn Christchurch is fairly basic, but you come here to go out and enjoy Dublin's sights, the shopping and the vibrant nightlife.

Location: Jurys Inn Christchurch is facing historical Christchurch Cathedral and the Dublinia museum across the street. The West gate to Dublin Castle is a five minutes' walk away from the hotel's main entrance. Temple Bar, St Patrick's Cathedral, Trinity College and Grafton Street are all within easy walking distance and many of Dublin's main bus routes stop practically outside the hotel's front door.

Room Rates At Jurys Inn: The Jury's Inn Christchurch offers one type of room only. Rooms can accommodate from one up to three adults, or two adults and two children aged under 10. Please note that all rooms at Jurys Inn Christchurch are non smoking. Rooms start from €79.00 per room per night, excluding breakfast. Bed and breakfast for two is available from €99.00 per night.

Meeting And Function Rooms: Jurys Inns do not offer dedicated meeting facilities at their Christchurch premises. However, there are six meeting rooms available at the nearby Jurys Inn Custom House near the International Financial Services centre on the Northside of the city.

Facilities: Bedrooms have wired Internet access. WiFi is available in public rooms. The hotel offers a range of refreshments at the Il Barista coffee bar, the Innfusion restaurant and the Inntro bar.

<u>How To Get To Jurys Inn Christchurch:</u> The Aircoach bus service to and from Dublin Airport stops at College Street outside Trinity. From here you can walk to Jurys Inn Christchurch in 15 minutes or take the 123 bus from across the road on the corner of College Green and Suffolk Street. A single ticket on the Aircoach costs €7.00. A taxi from the airport will take a good 35 minutes, pending traffic and set you back €25.00 or more. Bus routes 123, 49, 50, 51, 54, 77 and 78 all stop near the hotel. The nearest stop on the Red Luas line is Four Courts on the other side of the River Liffey. Leave the hotel , cross over to Christchurch Cathedral and keep walking down the hill on Winetavern Street, over the bridge and past the 18th century courts of law on your left until you reach Chancery Street. The Luas stop is to your left.

Phone: +353 (0)1 454 0000
Fax: +353 (0)1 454 0012

Hotel Morgan Dublin

The Morgan is a stylish boutique hotel in Dublin's Temple Bar quarter. The hotel is bright and airy with minimalist decor and many playful touches. If you are looking for intimate and trendy accommodation in Dublin's city centre, the Morgan has it all.

<u>Location:</u> The Morgan is located in Fleet Street, a narrow cobbled lane on the fringes of Dublin's cultural and nightlife quarter Temple Bar. You are far enough away from the hustle and bustle of Temple Bar proper for The Morgan to offer quiet, relaxed accommodation, yet

close enough to the action to walk to some of the best nightlife in town. The hotel is only a short stroll away from famous Trinity College and the designer boutiques and shops of Grafton Street and surrounds.

Room Rates At The Morgan: Standard doubles with a queen size bed start from €110.00 per room per night, excluding breakfast. Deluxe rooms come with air conditioning, free standing bath, bathrobes and slippers and start from €140.00 per room per night. Suites sleeping one or two adults and offering a lounge and kitchenette are available from €210.00 per night.

Meeting And Function Rooms: The Morgan has 6 dedicated meeting rooms that can accommodate between 2 and 60 delegates. All rooms are stylishly furnished, have plenty of natural daylight, WiFi Internet access and 46" plasma screens. Room hire for the full day starts from €300.00 at The Morgan.

Facilities: The Morgan bar is a popular haunt for fashionistas roaming the cobbled lanes of Temple Bar. The latest minimal chic and minimal music set the ambience in one of the places to be seen in Temple Bar. You can actually purchase mix CDs here, based on The Morgan's playlist. The hotel restaurant serves authentic Spanish Tapas from 12:00 daily. Secure parking at reduced rates is available for hotel guests at the Fleet Street car park.

How To Get To The Morgan: There is a taxi rank right in front of The Morgan Hotel. A taxi to or from the airport will take approximately 35 minutes and cost about €25.00 each way. The Aircoach bus service to and from Dublin airport passes through Westmoreland Street and charges €7.00 for a single journey. Just ask the driver to let you off near the corner of Westmoreland Street and Fleet Street. Westmoreland Street is served by a number of bus routes, including the 123 which will connect you with many of Dublin's visitor attractions. The nearest DART station is Tara Street, which is located a five minutes' walk away on the River Liffey.

Taxi rank just outside the arrivals hall at the Airport and taxi costs approx €25 each way

Phone: +353 (0)1 643 7000
Fax: +353 (0)1 643 7060,
E-mail: reservations@themorgan.com

Hotel Morrison Dublin

The Morrison is a beacon of Irish design among city centre hotels. Furnished in a minimalist style with light Asian touches by Irish fashion and interior design icon John Rocha in 1999, the hotel has recently been refurbished and expanded. The Morrison is still the only boutique hotel on the Northside of Dublin.

Location: The Morrison overlooks one of the most picturesque stretches of the River Liffey between Millennium Bridge and Grattan

Bridge. There is a boardwalk at water level running along the Liffey right in front of the hotel and the pedestrian-only Millennium Bridge offers great views over the city, up and down the river. The Morrison is very conveniently located for the Henry Street shopping district. Temple Bar and Dublin Castle are literally just on the other side of the river.

Room Rates At The Morrison: Standard doubles with queen size bed start from €135.00 per night per room excluding breakfast. Executive Rooms with king size bed are available from €160.00 per night per room. Breakfast is optional and can be booked ahead for €15.00 per person. Suites at the Morrison range from €285.00 to €1,335.00 for the Penthouse Suite with its wrap around balcony, Jacuzzi bath and great views over Dublin.

Meeting And Function Rooms: The Morrison has six airy, bright meeting rooms with a modern, minimalist feel and top notch audio visual equipment. The hotel can cater for groups from 2 to 240 delegates. All meeting rooms at the Morrison have natural daylight and can be accessed via a private entrance, separate from the general hotel lobby. Some of the meeting rooms have access to a private courtyard garden. Please contact the Morrison directly for room hire rates and special delegate packages.

Facilities: The ground floor bar at the Morrison is a landmark on the quays and attracts a young, trendy clientele. The Halo restaurant at the Morrison serves up modern Irish cooking with a hint of Asian fusion. The hotel also features a spa centre which offers a wide range of treatments and massages. All rooms have complimentary broadband Internet access and either an iPod docking stations or a CD player. Some rooms also offer Apple Mac PCs, LCD screens and surround sound systems. Nintendo Wii gaming consoles are available for hotel guests on request.

<u>How To Get To The Morrison:</u> A taxi from Dublin airport to The Morrison will take approximately 30 minutes, pending traffic. A single journey will cost about €25.00. The 'Jervis' stop on the Red Luas tram line is a short five minutes' walk from the hotel

Phone: +353 (0)1 887 2400
Fax: +353 (0)1 874 4039
E-mail: info@morrisonhotel.ie

Hotel O'Callaghan Stephen's Green

With its dark wood, open fireplaces, leather armchairs, the O'Callaghan Stephen's Green Hotel has a strong Irish traditional feel. The hotel stretches across four Georgian town houses and a modern glass atrium. Playwright George Fitzmaurice lived in one of the houses which are now part of the hotel. The O'Callaghan group owns three other hotels in Dublin: The Davenport, the Alexander and the Montclair All located on nearby Merrion Square.

Location: The O'Callaghan Stephen's Green Hotel is located on the corner of Harcourt Street and Cuffe Street, opposite the South-Western corner of St. Stephen's Green, Dublin's lavish city centre park. The hotel is a five minutes' walk away from Dublin's premier shopping district around Grafton Street. Many of Dublin's most popular restaurants as well as the nightlife on Camden Street and Wexford Street are practically on the hotel's doorstep.

Room Rates: Double rooms at the O'Callaghan Stephen's Green Hotel start from €135.00 per room per night, excluding breakfast. Junior Suites are available from €185.00 per night. Broadband Internet access is available but will be charged separately.

Meeting and Function Rooms: The O'Callaghan Stephen's Green has 7 meeting rooms which can accommodate between 10 and 40 delegates. The hotel also has a fully restored Georgian library, which is available for cocktail receptions and similar events. The meeting rooms are located in the historic part of the hotel and some feature open fireplaces and original stucco ceilings. All rooms benefit from natural daylight.

Facilities: The Pie Dish Bistro at the O'Callaghan Stephen's Green Hotel offers traditional Irish cooking. Room service is available around the clock. All rooms have flat screen LCD TVs and feature US and European type AC sockets.

How To Get To The O'Callaghan Hotel: A taxi from Dublin airport to the O'Callaghan Hotel will take approximately 40 minutes and cost about €30.00 for a single journey. Alternatively, you can take the Aircoach bus service to and from Dublin airport. The Aircoach stops across the road from the hotel at Lucent House and a single adult ticket is €7.00 for the journey. The Green Luas tram line passes in front of the hotel with stops conveniently located towards St. Stephen's Green and further down Harcourt Street.

Phone: +353 (0)1 607 3600
Fax: +353 (0)1 661 5663
E-mail: info@ocallaghanhotels.com

Hotel Westbury Dublin

Located off Dublin's main shopping mile, Grafton Street, The Westbury offers modern five star accommodation in a lively yet surprisingly private city centre location. The Westbury has been a Dublin institution for family lunches and get-togethers for years. With a total refurbishment completed at the beginning of 2009, the hotel is now presenting a fresh look.

Location: The Westbury is tucked away just off Grafton Street in Balfe Street. The Westbury is a haven for serious shoppers. Ideally located for Dublin's finest shops around Grafton Street and adjacent Clarendon Street, South William Street and Drury Street, the hotel building even houses its own exclusive shopping centre, the Westbury

Mall. The Gaiety Theatre is a 5 minutes' stroll away and many of Dublin's most popular pubs and restaurants are within easy reach.

Room Rates At The Westbury: Double rooms at the Westbury start from €189.00 per room per night, excluding breakfast. Breakfast is available at an extra charge of €15.00 per person when booked in advance together with the room. Suites have modern four poster king size beds and are available from €304.00 per night. The Presidential Suite features a private sauna, steam room and gym and is available from €879.00 per night.

Meeting And Function Rooms: The Westbury has 7 meeting rooms which can cater for up to 50 delegates. In addition, the hotel's main function room, the Grafton Suite, can accommodate up to 200 guests for receptions or events. Please contact the hotel directly for room hire rates.

Facilities: The Wilde restaurant offers traditional Irish cooking using prime local beef and fish from the Irish coastal waters. Or why not skip dinner and settle instead for a sumptuous afternoon Tea in The Gallery, watching the hustle and bustle of Grafton Street below. The Westbury's Marble Bar is decorated in a decadent Art Nouveau style and provides a stylish setting for drinks into the early morning hours. All bedrooms have complimentary high-speed Internet access, iPod docking stations, Nespresso coffee makers and Blackberry chargers.

How To Get To The Westbury: A taxi from Dublin airport to The Westbury will take approximately 40 minutes and cost about €30.00 for a single journey. The Aircoach bus service to and from Dublin airport stops at the top of Grafton Street which is a good 10 minutes' walk from the hotel. A single adult ticket is €7.00 for the journey. The nearest Luas tram stop is the Green Luas stop at St. Stephen's Green, a five minutes' walk away from The Westbury.

Phone: +353 (0)1 679 1122
Fax: +353 (0)1 679 7078
E-mail: westbury@doylecollection.com

Hotel Westin Dublin

The Westin is located in an opulent 19th century bank building in the centre of Dublin. The Westin is one of Dublin's newest hotels yet the look is firmly rooted in old world style. Dark wood and old fashioned comforts dominate the bedrooms while the public rooms make good use of the restored splendour of the building.

Location: The Westin Hotel is located on the corner of Westmoreland Street and College Green, overlooking the historic Bank Of Ireland building across Westmoreland Street which housed the Irish Parliament until the Act Of Union moved it to Westminster, London, in the year 1800. The hotel's neighbour across College Green is Dublin's historic Trinity College. The Temple Bar area starts literally on the opposite side of the road from the Hotel's main entrance and Dublin's main shopping mile, Grafton Street, is only a five minutes' stroll away.

Room Rates At The Westin: Doubles have queen size beds and start from €199.00 per room per night, excluding breakfast. Bed and breakfast for two people sharing starts from €224.00 per night. Junior Suites are available from €329.00 per night, excluding breakfast. High speed Internet access is available in all bedrooms and will be charged separately.

Meeting And Function Rooms: The Westin offers 7 meeting rooms catering for groups from 8 to 94 delegates. In addition, the hotels main function room, the Banking Hal from 1863l, can accommodate up to 250 guests. Delegate packages include room hire, lunch in the Exchange Restaurant, teas and coffees as well as use of in-room audio visual equipment and free WiFi for the duration of your meeting. Half day delegate packages are available from €60.00 per person and full day packages from €77.00 per delegate.

Facilities: Spa services including facials and massages are available to hotel guests in their own bedrooms. The Westin offer 24-hour room service and features a gym with full workout facilities which may be used by guests around the clock.

How To Get To The Westin: A taxi from Dublin airport to the Westin will take about 35 minutes in average traffic and charge approximately €25.00. The Aircoach shuttle bus to and from Dublin airport stops close to the Westin on Westmoreland Street. A single journey on the Aircoach costs €7.00 per adult. The closest DART station is Tara Street and can be reached by foot in 10 minutes. The nearest Luas tram stop is the Red Luas line stop in Lower Abbey Street across the River Liffey.

Phone: +353 (0)1 645 1000
Fax: +353 (0)1 645 1403
E-mail: reservations.dublin@westin.com

Getting Around in Dublin

Dublin's city centre is relatively small in size and you could stroll from the GPO to Stephens Green in under an hour, taking in the sights on the way.

A handy hint if you are trying to locate an address, postal codes are always odd numbers on the Northside and even numbers on the Southside. As a rule of thumb, the higher the number, the further away the location will be from the city centre.

If you would like to cover some distance, then Dublin has a good public transport network with a choice of buses, two tram lines (the Luas), a local area train running all the way along Dublin Bay (the Dart) and a large number of taxis.

Guided Tours

Dublin Bus Tours: The Dublin Bus Tour takes in most of the city centre sights. It is a 'hop-on, hop-off' affair, so you can get off the bus take a look around and get a later bus to the next stop. The Dublin Bus Tour costs €15. The separate 'South Coast & Gardens' tour brings you through Sandycove and Dalkey to the Powerscourt stately home and estate in the Wicklow Mountains and back. The 'North Coast & Castle' tour brings you out to the fishing port of Howth and to Malahide Castle.

Viking Splash Tours: See Dublin from the water as well as from the road, travelling in an American amphibian personnel carrier from World War II, a Dukw. The tour takes in the sites of Viking Dublin, the city's two famous cathedrals (St. Patrick's and Christchurch), Trinity College, Government Buildings and Georgian Dublin. The water leg of the tour brings you to the recording studio of U2 and explores the newly developed Grand Canal Docklands. Adult tickets cost €20.00, children's tickets are half price. For more information or to book tickets.: www.vikingsplash.ie

Making Your Own Way

Dublin by Bus: Dublin Bus (Bus Átha Cliath) operates a city-wide bus network. A typical city centre journey will cost you approximately €1.60 (€0.80 for children under 16). Bus drivers accept exact change only. If you plan to make more than the odd journey on the bus during your visit to Dublin you should consider purchasing a Rambler Ticket. A one day adult Rambler Ticket costs €6.00, a family ticket costs €10.00. Day tickets can be bought from the bus driver.

Dublin by Tram: Dublin has two tram lines called 'Luas'. The Red Luas line traverses the city from North East to South West and the Green Luas line connects St. Stephen's Green with the Southern suburbs. The Luas is a relatively recent arrival, and coaches are modern and spacious. Luas fares are roughly equivalent to bus fares.: www.luas.ie

Dublin by Train: There are a number of suburban and local trains that service several stops in the centre of Dublin and connect you with visitor attractions or accommodation in the suburbs. The most important local rail service is the DART, which traverses the city from North to South, travelling alongside Dublin Bay for most of the journey.

Dublin by Taxi: Dublin has a fair number of licensed taxi cabs which are marked by a yellow Taxi sign on top of their roof. The best way to get a taxi is to hail one down on the road. Taxis are, generally speaking, for hire if the yellow light is lit. But peek inside, sometimes the cabbie already has a fare on board but forgot to switch the light off. Dublin taxis are metered. An average journey in the city centre will cost between €6.00-10.00.

Dublin by Car: Getting around town by car is relatively easy outside rush hour. Generally speaking, rush hour is 7:00-9:00 and 16:00-19:00 Monday to Friday. Please note that major sporting matches can clog up the roads and available parking at weekends, so check before you go. The city centre is one big one-way system. A handy hint: The Quays on both sides of the Liffey operate in a clockwise circle! Imagine O'Connell Street as 12 o'Clock, Custom House as one o'clock, the International Financial Services Centre as two o'clock and so on. Remember TO DRIVE ON THE LEFT!

<u>Rental Cars</u>: Many major and international and local companies offer car rental in Dublin. The main car rental companies servicing Dublin are, in no particular order, Argus, Avis, Budget, Europcar, Hertz and Thrifty. The main pick up and drop off points for all car rentals are located at Dublin Airport, but many companies also offer city centre pick up and drop off.

<u>Dublin by Bicycle</u>: Dublin is great for cycling! For most parts, it is fairly flat with only a few modest climbs getting you anywhere. You can also park your ride everywhere. In many city centre locations you will find dedicated bicycle parking spots with chunky metal bars to chain your bike to. There are some dedicated cycle lanes around town. Bicycles are also allowed to use the bus lanes. Please note that you will share the bus lane with buses (obviously) but also taxis and motorcycles. The biggest danger to Dublin cyclists are, however, the humble pedestrians. Be aware that most pedestrians are blissfully unaware of bicycles and likely to step out right in front of you. Phoenix Park Bike Hire is the only dedicated bicycle hire place in Dublin. They offer 150 bikes, including some mountain bikes (ATBs) and racers

Dublin Bus Tour

There are several different types of buses on Dublin's roads. Dublin Bus (Bus Átha Cliath in Gaelic) with its fleet of yellow and blue liveried single and double-deckers gets you around town and to and from the suburbs. The white Bus Eireann coaches with the orange greyhound logo on the side connect you with other main Irish cities.

Tourist hop-on hop-off bus: An open top double decker bus will make sightseeing entertaining without having to go through the hassle of daily city life. These busses go around Dublins highlights in 8 to 20 minute intervals and you can get on and off as many times as you like. Meet fellow tourists and share your impressions. The bus runs daily all year round.

Getting Around Dublin By Bus: Dublin Bus (Bus Átha Cliath) is the main public transport provider. Its fleet of yellow and blue liveried buses carries 70% of all peak time public transport, which equals roughly half a million customers a day.

Bus Stops And Timetables: Bus stops are marked by a yellow pole crowned with a small yellow disc bearing the blue Dublin Bus logo. Distances between stops can vary significantly. In the city centre, they are usually quite close together. It is not unusual for a bus to stop every 150-200 metres on some routes.

If there is a timetable at your stop, take it as an indication of services only. The traffic in Dublin is quite heavy, particularly during rush hour from 7:00-9:00 and 16:00-19:00. There are some dedicated bus lanes, but they can mainly be found outside the city centre proper. If you are in a hurry, please factor this in and allow ample time to reach your destination.

Dublin Bus Fares: In Dublin you pay the driver. Fares are calculated in stages, the more stages between your starting point and your destination the higher the fare. A typical city centre journey will cost you approximately €1.60 (€0.80 for children under 16). The maximum fare is €4.50.

Some bus stops have tables displaying fares to different destinations from that particular stop. However, most bus stops don't divulge that sort of detail and Dubliners usually just state their destination and the driver will name the fare.

Make sure you have plenty of small change. Dublin Bus drivers are not required to accept notes and might refuse to let you on board. If you do not have the exact fare you will not get change from the driver. Instead, your ticket has a section that says 'Refund' and states the appropriate amount. If you want your change back, you need to head to the Dublin Bus office at 59 Upper O'Connell Street.

Rambler Ticket: If you plan to make more than the odd journey on the bus during your visit to Dublin you should consider purchasing a

Rambler Ticket. They are available for one day, three days, five days and seven days. A one day adult Rambler Ticket costs €6.00, a family ticket costs €10.00. Day tickets can be bought from the bus driver. You can buy longer term tickets online on the Dublin Bus homepage.: www.dublinbus.ie

Dublin Bus Etiquette: Dubliners queue at the bus stop, with the person who was there first nearest to the stop sign. If your stop services more than one bus line it is pefectly fine to jump the queue when the person in front of you is obviously not waiting for your bus. You enter and leave a bus through the front door by the driver only. You will notice many passengers muttering a 'thank you' to the driver when leaving the bus. If your bus has a middle door, do not bother to queue up in front of it, your driver will most likely not open it and you have to face a mad dash to the front of the bus to make your stop.

Going Long Distance: Bus Eireann coaches start and terminate at the Busaras or central bus terminal at Store Street on the North Quays near the International Financial Services Centre. Apart from connecting you with all major cities in Ireland, Bus Eireann also offers day trips to locations near Dublin, such as the megalithic tombs at Newgrange and the early Christian monastery and picturesque mountain lakes at Glendalough. Please see the Bus Eireann homepage for more information on daytrips:.www.buseireann.ie

Dublin by Train

Trains in Ireland are operated by Iarnród Éireann, a subsidiary of state transport company CIE, which also owns Dublin Bus and the overland coach network Bus Éireann. The greater Dublin area is serviced by a number of trains to and from other Irish cities as well as Belfast in Northern Ireland. The train services that are going to be most useful for travelling within the Dublin area are the DART, the Kildare Suburban Service or Arrow and the Western Suburban Service.

The Arrow train : The Arrow, or Kildare Suburban Service operates between Dublin and Kildare. The Arrow is the only train connection between Connolly and Tara Street to Heuston Station in the South of the city, which is a convenient stop for the Irish Museum Of Modern Art, the Guinness Storehouse and the National Museum Of Ireland - Decorative Arts & History. The next stop after Heuston is the large Park West office park. Suburban rail tickets are priced slightly higher than DART tickets and must be purchased at the rail station you are commencing your journey at.

The DART train: The DART, short for Dublin Area Rapid Transit, is a local area train that crosses the Dublin from North to South, stopping at a number of city centre locations. The full length of the DART line stretches from the fishing port of Howth in the North to the seaside commuter town of Greystones in the South. City centre stops are (from North to South): Connolly, Tara Street, Pearse Street and Grand

Canal Dock. Single tickets for a journey between city centre stops cost €1.65 for adults and €0.85 for children. Return tickets are €2.80 for adults and €1.45 for children. The maximum fare for a journey along Dublin Bay from Howth to Greystones is €8.00 return for adults and €3.30 for children.

<u>The Western Suburban Service:</u> The Western Suburban train departs from Connolly Station in the city centre and stops at Drumcondra, a popular suburb for Bed & Breakfast accommodation, as well as Phoenix Park. This makes the Western service convenient for reaching Dublin Zoo as well as the extensive, leafy landscape of Phoenix Park, one of the largest inner city parks in Europe. The journey from Connolly to Phoenix Park takes approximately 15 minutes. Watch out for your stop, the Western train does go all the way across the country to Sligo on the West coast of Ireland.

Dublin Taxi

It has become increasingly easy to find a taxi in Dublin in the last few years. Following changes to taxi licensing regulations in 2000, the number of taxis in Dublin has rocketed from 2,000 to 25,000, according to estimates by Dublin taxi drivers. It is still advisable to book a taxi to Dublin airport in advance if you have to be on a red eye flight from Monday to Friday but otherwise you should be able to pick up a taxi easily enough, if you know where to look. Here you find some tips for the best spots to hail a taxi in Dublin as well as information on taxi fares and phone numbers for the main Dublin taxi companies.

Taxis And Hackney Cabs: There are two types of taxis in Dublin: Licensed taxis and hackney cabs. You can hail a licensed taxi at a taxi rank or on the street while a hackney cab must be hired by phone or in person at a hackney office. A licensed taxi must display a yellow TAXI display panel on the top of the car's roof while hackney cabs are generally unmarked. Taxis are metered while hackney offices will have a fixed price list for different destinations or you haggle out a price in advance of your journey. The difference in the final cost is usually negligible these days. During rush hour, licensed taxis can use Dublin bus lanes but Hackney's can't. Hackney offices are usually small walk-in shops on main streets, particularly in Dublin suburbs, with names featuring 'Cars' or 'Cabs'. You may also find business cards with a number for a hackney in pubs, bars and Bed & Breakfasts.

Taxi Fares: The initial charge when you hail a Dublin taxi is €4.10 and includes the first kilometre. Additional kilometres are charged at €1.03. The kilometre rate goes up to €1.35 after 15 kilometres. On longer journeys, the rate increases again to €1.77 per kilometre. Bear that in mind when taking a taxi to or from locations on the outskirts of Dublin. If you are travelling in a group of two or more, then your driver will add a €1.00 charge per additional passenger. Children under 12 count as half an adult. Between 20:00 and 8:00 you can expect to pay approximately 10% on top of the daytime rates. If you are travelling to the airport, it is advisable to agree a fee in advance. If you order a taxi by phone, most companies will be happy to quote a fixed price for airport transfers or other, longer journeys. All taxi fares are set by the Irish taxi regulator, the Commission For Taxi Regulation. The last fare increase took place on 1 November 2008 and all fares stated here reflect this latest tariff.

Taxi Ranks: There are currently 79 taxi ranks in Dublin which are in service 24 hours a day. The main taxi ranks in the city centre are located on O'Connell Street, up towards Parnell Square and on College Green opposite the Bank Of Ireland and the main gate into Trinity College. Additional night time taxi ranks operate between 20:00 and 6:00 on several locations in the city centre, including Dame Street and Merrion Row.

Taxis By Night: The queues at taxi ranks typically swell by night, particularly after the pubs close. Your best bet is to hail a taxi down on the street. Good spots to find an empty taxi are the main runs cabbies use returning into town after dropping off a fare. Around the city centre, try the North Quays like Arran Quay, Inns Quay and Ormond Quay. If you are further down on the Southside, try Camden Street, Wexford Street or South Great Georges Street.

North City Centre: The North quays of the River Liffey are always a good bet to hail a taxi on the street. Competition by fellow travellers is fierce, so pick a place early on between Queen Street and the Four Courts on the North Quays. O'Connell Street has a large taxi rank opposite the Savoy cinema. A lesser known spot to pick up a taxi is Sackville Street off O'Connell Street, further down towards the Liffey. There is usually a line of taxis waiting here for a call or a free spot at the rank up the road.

South City Centre: South Great Georges Street is a good place to hail a taxi on the road if you are in the town centre. Late at night you may have to venture further down the road towards Wexford Street to avoid the crowds of potential taxi customers spilling out of the pubs here. One of Dublin's main taxi ranks is on College Green, just in front of the gates to Trinity College. The queue here is fast moving during shopping hours, but at night the queue tends to grow longer and longer. Move around the corner of Trinity towards Dawson Street. There is a taxi rank on Dawson Street outside the Cafe En Seine. But queues here can be lengthy and you might wander down the road towards Stephen's Green to catch an incoming taxi.

Dublin Taxi Companies: Below you find the telephone numbers for the main taxi companies servicing Dublin. Call centres are usually open 24 hours. Waiting times may differ, pending traffic conditions and time of the day. If you can, avoid ordering a taxi at peak times between 7:00 and 9:00 and 16:00 and 19:00 from Monday to Friday. If you are thinking of going out on a Saturday night, it is advisable to book your taxi before 18:00 that day. At other times you can expect to wait 20-30 minutes from putting in a call to seeing your taxi arrive.

City Cabs: Phone: 01 872 7272. Metro Cabs: Phone: 01 668 3333. National Radio Cabs: Phone: 01 677 2222. Pony Cabs: Phone: 01 661 2233. Taxi 7: Phone: 01 460 0000. Xpert Digi Taxis: Phone: 01 667 0777

Dublin Car Rental

If you fancy yourself as a bit of a motorist, Dublin can be quite conveniently explored in a rental car. There is a choice of international and local car rental companies - Nearly all offering car pick up and drop off both in the city centre and at the airport. You pretty much get a standard selection of makes and models available throughout Europe. Many car rental companies offer optional on-board GPS navigation systems. Please note that, compared to other main European tourist destinations, you may find car rental relatively expensive in Ireland. It is advisable to shop around and book in advance to get a competitive price.

Please remember to DRIVE ON THE LEFT and avoid the rush hour between 7:00-9:00 and 16:00-19:00. Dublin is well signposted, with most signage being bi-lingual Irish and English. Don't worry, the English version is usually displayed more prominently.

Age Of Driver: Conditions vary slightly between rental companies with regard to the age of the driver. Most car rental companies in Ireland specify a minimum age, some have a maximum age for drivers as well. Where available, this information ah been added to the company profiles below. Generally speaking, if you are younger than 25 or older than 69, you may need to shop around a bit for a rental.

Driving Licence: To drive a rental car in Ireland, drivers must be in possession of a full, unendorsed driving licence which they have held for at least two years prior to the start of the rental period. The licence must have been issued by the country of your permanent residence. Holders of UK, US, Canadian, Australian and all EU member states do not need to supply an International Driving Permit (IDP). If you produce an IDP, you must also show your original domestic driving licence. UK residents with a photo card driving licence must show both parts of their current driving licence when picking up the car. Please note, that drivers must be in possession of their licence at all times when driving the rental car.

Dublin Car Hire Companies

Argus: Established in 1959, Argus Rent A Car is a family-run Irish company with office at Dublin Airport and on the Southside of the city. Argus' city location is at 59 Terenure Road East in Rathgar, Dublin 6, south of the Grand Canal.: www.argus-rentacar.com/dublin-car-rental.asp

Atlas: An Irish Car Hire company established in 1989, Atlas Car Hire are a local Dublin car rental company. Atlas has offices at Dublin Airport and in the city centre, close to the River Liffey at Lombard Street, Dublin 2. Atlas requires drivers to be at least 25 years of age.: www.atlascarhire.com/carhire-dublincitycenter.htm

Avis: Avis maintains car hire office at Dublin Airport and on Dublin's Southside in Kilmainham. The Kilmainham office is a short walk away from Heuston train station and the Heuston stop on the Red Luas tram route.: www.avis.ie/CarHire/Europe/Ireland/Dublin/Dublin-City-Centre

Budget: Budget is one of the larger players in Ireland with a fleet of 4,000 cars. Budget has offices at Dublin Airport and on the Northside of the city. Budget's city location is in Drumcondra, north east of Parnell Square at 151 Lower Drumcondra Road, Dublin 9. You will see the office on

the right hand side as you travel from the city centre. Budget requires drivers to be 23 or older to rent a car.: www.budget.ie/dublincity.htm

Europcar: Murray's Europcar is Ireland's longest established car hire company and has been in business for more than 50 years. Europcar has offices at Dublin Airport and in the city centre at 1 Mark Street, Off Pearse Street Dublin 2.: www.europcar.ie

Irish Car Rental: Irish Car Rental are the local agents for National and Alamo cars. The company has been in business for more than 25 years and operates a fleet of 2,500 vehicles. Irish Car Rentals maintain soffices at Dublin Airport and on the Southside at 7 Terenure Road

East in Rathgar, Dublin 6. Irish Car Rental requires drivers to be at least 25 years of age.: www.irishcarrentals.com/car_rental_dublin_city.html

Thrifty: Thrifty operates offices at Dublin Airport and in the city centre. Thrifty's city office is one of the most central car pick-up and drop-off locations, close to Trinity College and Pearse Street Dart station. When exiting the station turn right and cross Pearse Street. The Thrifty office is situated on your left hand side.: www.thrifty.ie/Dublin_city_downtown_car_rentals.php

Car Rental Comparison Site

Autoeurope: Why not let a price comparison site do the running around, compare prices and secure discounts on rental list prices for you? One such comparison site with a dedicated Irish web site is www.autoeurope.ie. Autoeurope scans Irish and international car hire companies for available rental deals on the dates and at the location you specify.: www.autoeurope.ie

Travel to Dublin

Dublin is located on the East Coast of Ireland, the last major island outpost of Europe before you hit the Atlantic and, eventually, the North American continent. To get to Dublin, you can either fly or take a ferry. If you are already on the island, Dublin is well connected by train, coach and a network of motorways.

Flights to Dublin: The city is serviced by only one airport, Dublin Airport. Dublin is one of the ten busiest airports in Europe with an average of 60,000 passengers per day, rising to 80,000 during the peak season. Many international airlines fly to Dublin Airport. As of January 2009, Dublin airport was served by 78 airlines on more than 200 routes. For an up to date overview of available connections, please see the Dublin Airport.

Air Travel Times

Approximate travel times to Dublin by air are, pending weather conditions:

UK Airports: 45 mins
European Airports: 2-2.5h
Scandinavian Airports: 3h
Eastern European Airports: 4h
New York: 5.5h
Other Intercontinental: 8+h

Travelling To/From Dublin Airport: Dublin city centre is accessible from the airport by bus and taxi. The journey from Dublin Airport to the city centre takes approximately 45 minutes. Both buses and taxis use special lanes and can avoid the worst of the traffic. prices for a journey into the city centre by bus start from €6.00. A taxi fare to a city centre location will set you back approximately €25.00.

Rental Car: Many international and national car rental companies are located in the arrivals hall of Dublin Airport. Please note that, compared to other main European tourist destinations, you may find car rental relatively expensive in Ireland. It is advisable to shop around and book in advance to get a competitive price.

Please remember to DRIVE ON THE LEFT in Ireland! Travelling by car from Dublin Airport into the city takes approximately 45 minutes, pending on the time of day. If you can, avoid the rush hour between 7:00-9:00 and 16:00-19:00. The route is well signposted. If you are travelling to a location on Dublin's Southside, you will likely save time using the Port Tunnel and the East Link, both are tolled but help you bypass city centre traffic.

Dublin by Ferry: Dublin has two major ferry ports, Dublin Port and Dun Laoghaire (pronounced 'Doon Leerie'). Both ports are serviced several times a day from Holyhead in Wales. There are two principal ferry lines operating on the Holyhead-Dublin route, Stena Line and Irish Ferries. Both offer a standard 3.5 hour and a faster 2 hour crossing on high speed catamarans, sea conditions permitting. Please not that this is no idle threat, if the Irish Sea gets rough, the catamarans stay in port and only the slow boat goes. It is advisable to contact your ferry line on the day you travel and confirm your sailing time.

Ferry Travel Times: Stena offers a 2h service to Dun Laoghaire and a 3:15h to Dublin Port. Irish Ferries operates a 2h and a 3.5h service, both to Dublin Port.

www.stenaline.co.uk/ferry/routes/holyhead-dublin/

www.irishferries.com/routes-times-dublin-holyhead.asp

Dublin Port: Dublin Port is located on the Northside of the city, approximately 3km from the centre. If you travel as a foot passenger, there is a public bus service that brings you to the central bus terminal in the centre, the Busaras near the International Financial Services Centre. If you are travelling by car to destinations outside the city centre, you can use the tolled Port Tunnel to connect with the M50 ring road and the main airport and Belfast road, the M1. www.dublinporttunnel.ie

Dun Laoghaire Port: Dun Laoghaire is situated on the Southside, circa 11km from the city centre. Travelling from Dun Laoghaire into the city as a foot passenger, you have a choice of buses and the DART local railway, which calls at many stops convenient for city centre locations.

Both Dublin Port and Dun Laoghaire are linked by the East Link toll bridge, which helps you avoid city centre traffic if you travel by car.

Dublin By Train: The main railway line through Ireland runs North-South along the East Coast, connecting Dublin with Cork at the very southern tip of Ireland and Belfast in Northern Ireland.

From Belfast: Travelling from Belfast in Northern Ireland, you can get to Dublin on the Translink Enterprise. The Enterprise travels several times a day. Fares start from as little as £10.00 for an adult day return.

Travel time is approximately 2.5h. If you take an early service, you can get an Ulster Fry hot breakfast on the train for a surcharge. It's worth a thought, if you are going to be sightseeing or shopping all day. The Enterprise arrives at Connolly Station on Dublin's Northside. Connolly is situated on the Red Luas tram line and is serviced by a large number of buses. The central bus station, Busaras, is literally opposite the train station.

From Cork: Getting from Cork to Dublin by train is approximately a 4h journey. A day return starts at €71 for Adults. There are special family tickets and other discounts available. The Cork train arrives at Heuston Station on Dublin's Southside. Heuston is located on the Red Luas tram line that brings you into the city centre and connects with Connolly station. www.irishrail.ie

Dublin by Coach: Bus Eireann connects most major towns across Ireland with Dublin. Bus Eireann coaches start and terminate at the Busaras or central bus terminal at Store Street on the North Quays near the International Financial Services Centre. www.buseireann.ie

Dublin by Car: There is a saying in Ireland that all roads lead to Dublin. Ireland's single largest metropolis is well connected to the rest of the country by a network of motorways and National Routes. The M50 ringroad makes it easy to navigate around the city.

M50 Toll Road: Please note that the M50 is a toll road, but you can use large chunks of it for free, depending on the direction you are travelling in. The toll point is located between the exits for the N3 and the N4 on the north-eastern tranche of the M50. Please note that tolling is barrier-less: If you travel in a rental car, check with your rental company how M50 tolls are billed. If you travel in a private car you are expected to pay online by 20:00 the next calendar day. www.eflow.ie

Dublin Airport

Dublin Airport is Ireland's main international air hub, lying ten kilometres north of Dublin City Centre. Ranking among the Top 10 busiest airports in Europe, Dublin handles both domestic and international flights and has all the facilities you would expect from a major international airport, such as currency exchange, lost property office and baby-changing facilities.

Flights To Dublin Airport: Dublin Airport is served by 63 airlines as of January 2011. Direct flights are available from most major airports in the UK, continental Europe and some key airports in the US. Flights from other overseas territories typically require a changeover in London (UK) or Frankfurt (Germany).

Dublin Airport Arrivals: The Arrivals lounge contains 10 luggage carousels. A screen informs passengers on arrival where to collect their baggage. Customer service and information desks are easily located and can advise on Dublin hotels and travel options into the city. There is a Bank of Ireland currency exchange desk in the baggage reclaim hall available from 06:00 to 22:30. Other ATMs and car rental services are available on exiting customs. Please note, that there is a limited choice of food and drink outlets in the Arrivals area.

Car Rental: Car rental services are available in both terminals at Dublin Airport. In Terminal 1, the car rental desks are located in the main arrivals hall and easy to find. In Terminal 2, signs guide travellers the short distance to the car rental desks. From this point, staff for the various rental companies will guide you to their bus service which will bring you the short distance to the car rental depot located on the grounds of Dublin Airport. With regard to car rental at Dublin Airport, the following companies are in operation: Hertz, Europcar, CARHIRE.ie, Irish Car Rentals (part of Europcar), Avis, Enterprise and Dan Dooley

Left Luggage: Please note, that there are no baggage lockers in the airport. A left luggage facility operates in the car park atrium across the road from the main terminal building. The left luggage facility is open between 06:00 and 23:00.

Internet Access: Dublin Airport offers internet access via dedicated pay-as-you-go internet kiosks and WiFi. There is a charge to use WiFi and you need to prepay. There are several WiFi time vending machines in the Departures area and near the gates. You can also buy WiFi time at most cafes and bars in the airport. In Arrivals, you can purchase WiFi time at the Uppercrust Cafe, the J Bar and most food outlets on the Mezzanine level.

Check-In: Dublin Airport is currently undergoing major expansion and modernisation work. It is also very busy, with up to 80,000 passengers moving through the airport every day. It is advisable that you give yourself ample time to check in. Most airlines operating from Dublin Airport recommend that you check in 90 minutes prior to your cheduled departure time. Check-in desks typically open two hours before scheduled departure.

Dublin Airport Departures: The Departures area offers a multitude of facilities for travellers waiting for flights out of Dublin. These include business lounges and a wide range of shopping outlets offering traditional Irish goods such as smoked salmon, cheeses and handmade chocolates, as well as books, fashion and Irish music CDs and DVDs. Excellent bars are located in each of the departure piers. The main departure area offers a range of several cafes and self-service restaurants.

Getting To/From Dublin City Centre: The city centre is accessible from the airport by bus and taxi via the M1 Dublin-Belfast motorway and the M50 ring road. Taxis are well-regulated with despatchers on duty to minimise queue disruption.

Taxis: To reach the taxi rank, leave Arrivals through the main exit doors and turn right. **Taxis** are metered and a ride to a city centre location should cost approximately €25. Please note, that there are extra charges for baggage.

Bus Connections to/From Dublin Airport

<u>Airlink</u>: Dublin Bus (also signposted as Bus Átha Cliath in Gaelic) operates two Airlink lines connecting Dublin Airport with the city centre. The 747 brings you to the main thoroughfare on the Northside, O'Connell Street, and to the central bus station Busaras. The 748 travels further along the quays and terminates at Heuston train station on the Southside, near the Guinness Brewery. Bus services operate directly outside Arrivals.

The journey from Dublin Airport to the city centre takes approximately 45 minutes. Airlink tickets cost €6.00 Single and €10.00 return (children travel for half the price) and can be bought at the Bus and Rail information desk and the Dublin Tourism information desk in the arrivals hall at Dublin Airport. Tickets can also be bought from vending machines located at the bus departure points on the arrivals road outside the terminal. www.dublinbus.ie

<u>Aircoach</u>: The company's blue coaches are easily recognisable outside the main terminal building, close to the Dublin Bus services. Route 1 serves St Stephen's Green, Fitzwilliam Square, Merrion Square, Ballsbridge and Donnybrook and major hotels along the way. Route 2 operates between the airport and the city centre connecting with

Leopardstown, Sandyford and Stillorgan and other suburbs to the south of the city.

Aircoach tickets cost €7.00 Single and €12.00 Return to and from city centre locations. Children pay a standard €1.50 Single fare. The Aircoach services a large number of locations on Dublin's Southside, all the way out to the seaside town of Greystones in Wicklow, just beyond Dublin Bay. The maximum fare for adults is €13 Single and €20 Return. www.aircoach.ie

Local Bus Routes: There are other, cheaper local bus services that will take you into the city centre. These include the 16, 41, 46x and the 102, although these services can take considerably longer. The 16/16a also connects with Drumcondra station which is on the main Maynooth-Connolly line. The journey takes about 15 minutes, pending traffic.

Additionally, Urbus operate services from the airport to nearby suburbs Castleknock and Blanchardstown.

Flights to Dublin, Ireland

More and more airlines are flying to Dublin airport each year and Ireland's second carrier, Ryanair, is continually expanding its services into Europe. For visitors to Dublin, this means it is easier than ever to visit Ireland's capital city.

Thanks to Ireland's close historic ties with the USA, there are scheduled direct flights to Dublin from seven major US airports. Dublin is one of the few airports offering 'border preclearance' services for US-bound passengers.

For long distance destinations in Asia, Africa or South and Central America, you may need to change over at one of London's airports (Heathrow, Gatwick, Stansted, Luton or City), or with another major European air terminal, such as Frankfurt, Munich, Paris (Charles De Gaulle) or Amsterdam. There are around 50 scheduled flights daily from Dublin to all five London airports for onward connections to overseas destinations.

Below you will find some scheduled direct flights to Dublin. The list focuses on the busiest all-year-round routes to and from Dublin. Many airlines add direct flights from other European airports to Dublin during the summer months. Check before you go.

Irish Airlines

Aer Lingus: Ireland's national carrier is Aer Lingus. The airline flies to destinations all over the world with direct flights to many major airports in the USA and Canada. Aer Lingus has re-styled itself as a budget airline in recent years, competing with Ryanair on some routes: www.aerlingus.com

Ryanair: Ireland's other big airline is the budget carrier, Ryanair. Ryanair regularly add new routes to regional airports throughout

Europe, often with good deals from smaller airports.: www.ryanair.com

Aer Arann: The smallest Irish carrier, Aer Arann operates a range of domestic flights to Dublin from Cork, Donegal, Galway, Sligo and Knock, as well as international flights from the Isle of Man, Blackpool, Cardiff and Inverness in the UK.: www.aerarran.com

Flights to Dublin

Flights to Dublin from France: Paris is an important air hub for flights to and from Dublin and serviced by three different airlines.

Paris airport Charles De Gaulle is a significant hub for intercontinental connection flights to and from Dublin. Airfares to Dublin from France are cheap thanks to the competition between airlines, particularly Ryanair and Aer Lingus.

Aer Lingus: Irish airline Aer Lingus operates daily flights from Paris Charles De Gaulle to Dublin. Aer Lingus offers cheap airfares, reserved seating and convenient online booking. www.aerlingus.com

Cityjet: City Jet, a subsidiary of French national carrier Air France, flies daily to Dublin from Paris Charles De Gaulle airport. City Jet flies up to seven times a day to Dublin Airport, giving you maximum flexibility. www.cityjet.com

<u>Ryanair</u>: Budget carrier Ryanair flies directly to Dublin from Beauvais-Tille, 80km to the north of Paris. There is a coach transfer to and from Paris which takes approximately 1 hour. Ryanair also services a number of regional airports all over France. Some of these routes are only flown in the summer, such as Biarritz, Carcassonne, Marseille and La Rochelle. Ryanair often has special deals on flight tickets to Dublin. Please note that Ryanair allocates seats on the plane on a first-come-first-served basis. www.ryanair.com

Flights to Dublin from Germany: Frankfurt Airport is a main connecting hub for intercontinental flights to Dublin. Many regional airports offer directflights to Dublin as well.

One of Ireland's main trade partners on the continent, Germany is the second busiest source of air traffic with Ireland after the UK. Frankfurt am Main is the main airport, with daily flights to Dublin. Frankfurt is the main hub for intercontinental air travel to Dublin after London Heathrow.

<u>Aer Lingus</u>: Irish airline Aer Lingus operates direct flights from to Dublin from Frankfurt, Munich and Duesseldorf. Refreshments are charged extra on board. Flying with Aer Lingus, you usually get a shorter walk from your plane at Dublin airport. Aer Lingus has restyled itself as a low cost airline in recent years and often has discounted airfares from Germany to Dublin when you book online. www.aerlingus.com

Lufthansa: German national carrier Lufthansa services Dublin Airport from its Frankfurt base. Lufthansa often has very good deals on flights to Dublin, particularly if you book at least a month in advance. The cabin crew serves refreshments on the 2 hour flight. Flying with Lufthansa, you typically have more check-in options and a shorter walk to your plane at Frankfurt. www.lufthansa.com

Ryanair: Irish budget carrier Ryanair offers daily direct flights from Duesseldorf. Ryanair also flies direct to Dublin from regional airports such as Frankfurt Hahn, which is located roughly halfway between Cologne and Frankfurt, and Bremen. Ryanair often advertises special offers on airfares to Dublin. Like with many other low cost airlines, you pay taxes, baggage handling fees and airport charges on top of that. www.ryanair.com

German Wings: German budget airline German Wings offer direct flights to Dublin from regional airports such as Dresden, Leipzig or Cologne/Bonn to Dublin in the summer months. www.germanwings.com

Flights to Dublin from Italy: Both Aer Lingus and Ryanair are operating direct flights to Dublin from Rome and Milan.

Rome and Milan are the main Italian cities servicing Dublin. Between the two cities, you have a choice of five airports with daily connections to Dublin Airport.

Aer Lingus: Aer Lingus flies directly to Dublin from Rome Fiumicino. You can also travel directly to Dublin with Aer Lingus from either Linate or Malpensa airport near Milan in the north of Italy. Aer Lingus has dropped its prices recently and offers low cost tickets with the comfort of reserved seating. www.aerlingus.com

Ryanair: Ryanair operates daily flights from Rome Ciampino and from Orio Al Serio airport near Milan. The airline also flies directly to Dublin from Venice in the North East of Italy. The carrier operates additional routes between Dublin and regional Italian airports in the summer months. Ryanair is a low cost airline that often has particularly cheap flights to Dublin. You book your flight online and do not require a ticket to check in, just your reservation number. Seats on Ryanair flights are allocated on first-come-first-served basis when you board the plane. www.ryanair.com

Flights to Dublin from The Netherlands: The main departure point for flights from The Netherlands to Dublin is Amsterdam Schiphol.

Amsterdam Schiphol is the main airport servicing Dublin. There is only one other, regional airport with scheduled flights to Dublin and that is Eindhoven in the South-East of the country. Amsterdam airport Schiphol is a convenient air hub for intercontinental and European flights to and from Dublin.

Flights from Amsterdam to Dublin

Aer Lingus: Aer Lingus flies directly from Amsterdam Schiphol to Dublin. The Irish carrier recently restyled itself as a low cost airline and offers cheap flight tickets on the popular Amsterdam to Dublin route. Book online for the best flight tariffs. www.aerlingus.com

KLM: Dutch national airline KLM offers flights to Dublin with a brief stop-over in Manchester or Birmingham in the north of England. Both are relatively compact airports, so changing planes is typically hassle free. www.klm.com

Flights from Eindhoven to Dublin

Ryanair: Low cost airline Ryanair operates a direct flight from Eindhoven, the home of electronics giant Philips, in the South-East of the Netherlands to Dublin. Book online with this ticketless airline and take advantage of the cheap ticket prices.
www.ryanair.com

Filghts Dublin to Amsterdam: Detailed information on the vice-versa route, ie. from Dublin to Amsterdam.: www.amsterdam.info

Flights to Dublin from Poland: Direct flights are avaialble from Polish capital Warsaw as well as regional airports.

With a sizeable Polish expat community in Dublin, there are daily direct flights from Poland's capital city Warsaw to Dublin. Some regional airports offer direct flights as well.

<u>Aer Lingus</u>: Aer Lingus operates daily, direct flights on the Warsaw to Dublin route. Despite being the only carrier offering direct flights from Poland's capital Warsaw, Aer Lingus offers good deals on airfares to Dublin. Buy tickets online for the cheapest flights to Dublin with reserved seating. www.aerlingus.com

<u>Lot</u>: Polish airline Lot offers flights from a wide choice of regional airports throughout Poland. Flights to Dublin will require a brief stop-over at Frankfurt or Duesseldorf in Germany to change planes for Dublin. www.lot.com

<u>Ryanair</u>: Low cost airline Ryanair flies directly to Dublin from regional airports throughout Poland, including Szczecin and Wroclaw. Ryanair is a strictly no frills carrier - no reserved seating and extra charges for baggage - but tickets to Dublin often go very cheap. www.ryanair.com

Flights to Dublin from Portugal: Both Lisbon and Faro are directly connected with Dublin.

With Portugal having established itself as a favourite destination for Irish holiday home owners, golf fanatics and family holidaymakers alike, there are daily direct flights from Lisbon and Faro to Dublin.

<u>Aer Lingus</u>: Aer Lingus operates year-round Dublin routes from Portugal. The airline flies directly to Dublin from the Portuguese capital Lisbon and from the holiday hub of Faro in the South of the country. If you avoid times when Irish holidaymakers return to Dublin,

then you can get some really cheap plane tickets to Dublin. Aer Lingus has recently slashed prices in a move towards establishing itself as a budget airline. www.aerlingus.com

Ryanair: Ryanair operates several seasonal routes between Portugal and Dublin. The budget airline offers flights from Porto in the North of the Country during the summer. Tickets to Dublin often go very cheap, particularly when flights return empty after delivering Irish holidaymakers to Portuguese resorts. Ryanair is a no frills airline - baggage is charged extra and there are no reserved seats - but offers some of the keenest airfares around.
www.ryanair.com

Flights to Dublin from Spain: Direct flights to Dublin are available from Madrid, Barcelona and Malaga.

A number of Spanish airports offer direct flights to Dublin all year round. Madrid is the main airport servicing Dublin with a total of three carriers offering daily flights.

Aer Lingus: Aer Lingus offers direct flights to Dublin from Madrid, Barcelona in the East and Malaga in the South of the country. Book online for cheap flights by the recently re-styled budget airline. Aer Lingus offers low airfares with the comfort of pre-flight seat reservation. www.aerlingus.com

<u>Iberia</u>: Spanish national carrier Iberia flies directly to Dublin from its Madrid hub. Iberia operates an extensive network throughout Spain, putting Dublin within easy reach of virtually every part of mainland Spain, the Balearic Islands and the Canary Islands. www.iberia.com

<u>Ryanair</u>: Ryanair flies directly from Malaga and Murcia to Dublin. In the summer months, Ryanair also operates flights to Dublin from regional Spanish airports including Alicante, Reus and Valencia. Time your journey right and you can get bargain basement tickets on flights returning to Dublin after they delivered Irish holiday revellers in the sunny South. www.ryanair.com

Flights to Dublin from The UK: It is convenient and fast to fly to Dublin from Ireland's next door neighbour, The UK. All international and many regional UK airports offer daily flights to Dublin.

Historically, London has been Dublin's gateway to the rest of the world when it comes to air travel. There are more direct flights available to and from exotic locations these days, but the Dublin-London route remains very busy. Consequently, all five airports servicing the greater London area are directly connected with Dublin Airport. Of the five London airports, London Heathrow remains the main international air hub for intercontinental flights to and from Dublin. It is also a busy stop-over for flights to other European airports.

Aer Arann: Aer Arann, the smallest of the three Irish airlines, flies directly from Cardiff in Wales to Dublin. Aer Arann also operates flights to Dublin from the Isle Of Man. www.aerarann.com

Aer Lingus: Aer Lingus flies several times a day to Dublin from London Heathrow and London Gatwick. Aer Lingus has daily, scheduled flights to Dublin from Birmingham in the Midlands and Manchester in the North. The airline also flies directly to Dublin from the Scottish airports of Glasgow and Edinburgh. www.aerlingus.com

Bmi: UK airline bmi operates direct flights to Dublin from London Heathrow. If you are travelling to catch a rugby match in Dublin, remember that bmi is the official airline of the England Rugby team! www.flybmi.com

British Airways: UK national carrier British Airways offers several direct flights a day from both London Heathrow and London Gatwick. BA City Flyer, a subsidiary of British Airways, operates direct flights to Dublin from this airport, which is conveniently located for The City and the East End. www.britishairways.com

Ryanair: London Stansted serves as Ryanair's main air hub in Europe. The Irish budget carrier offers more routes and options from Stansted than from its Dublin home. Ryanair further offers some of its cheapest air fares from Stansted. You can often get real bargain flights to Dublin from here!

The airline also flies to Dublin from two other London airports, Gatwick and Luton.

Ryanair operates direct flights from a wide range of regional airports throughout England, Scotland and Wales. You can get daily direct flights at often keen prices from Birmingham in the Midlands and Manchester in the North, from Bristol in the South West and Newcastle in the North East as well as from Glasgow and Edinburgh in Scotland. www.ryanair.com

Flights to Dublin from The USA: Direct flights to Dublin are available from seven international airports in the US, including JFK, Boston, Chicago O'Hare, San Francisco and more.

Since the days when the Irish emigrated in thousands to the US in the absence of jobs or - during the 19th century famine - basic food at home, both countries have been joined by tight bonds. These days, you are more likely to see US citizens travelling to Ireland to trace their family roots and Dublin is well served from seven international airports in the US.

Aer Lingus: New York is the main US location servicing Dublin. Aer Lingus offers daily direct flights from New York John F Kennedy Airport to Dublin. Flights from JFK to Dublin take approximately 5.5 hours. Further south on the East Coast, Aer Lingus also flies directly from Boston to Dublin. Aer Lingus further operates daily flights to Dublin from San Francisco on the West Coast and from Chicago. A direct flight from Chicago O'Hare Airport to Dublin takes approximately 7.5 hours. The trip from San Francisco takes 10 hours. www.aerlingus.com

Continental Airlines: US airline Continental flies directly to Dublin from Newark Airport in New Jersey, which is conveniently located for New York. www.continental.com

Delta Airlines: US carrier Delta Airlines flies directly to Dublin from New York JFK. Delta also operates daily direct flights from Atlanta, Georgia, and Orlando, Florida, on the East Coast. www.delta.com

Flights to Dublin from The Baltic States: The three Baltic states - Estonia, Latvia and Lithuania - are well connected with Dublin. Air Baltic operates daily direct flights to Dublin from its Baltic hub in Riga (Latvia). Additional direct flights to Dublin are operated by Aer Lingus from Vilnius (Lithuania) and by Ryanair from Kaunas (Lithuania).: www.airbaltic.com. www.aerlingus.com. www.ryanair.com

Flights To Dublin From The Czech Republic: Aer Lingus operates direct flights from Prague to Dublin.: www.aerlingus.com

Flights To Dublin From Hungary: Both Malev, the national Hungarian carrier, and Aer Lingus fly directly to Dublin from Budapest. Budapest airport is also a convenient hub for many Eastern European and Middle Eastern destinations.: www.malev.com. www.aerlingus.com

Flights To Dublin From Luxembourg: Luxair operates daily scheduled flights from Luxembourg to Dublin.: www.luxair.lu

Flights To Dublin From The Middle East: There is a daily direct flight from Abu Dhabi in the United Arab Emirates to Dublin, operated by Etihad Airways, the national carrier of the United Arab Emirates. Flights from other airports in the Middle East require a changeover at one of the following air hubs: Frankfurt (Germany), Paris Charles De Gaulle (France), Amsterdam (Netherlands) or London Heathrow (UK).: www.etihadairways.com

Flights To Dublin From Russia: S7, formerly known as Sibir Airlines, offers direct flights from Moscow Domodedovo International Airport to Dublin in the summer months. The main air hub for connecting flights to Dublin from Russian airports is Frankfurt (Germany).: www.s7.ru

Flights To Dublin From Scandinavia: There are direct flights to Dublin from Copenhagen (with SAS), Oslo (with SAS or Ryanair) and Stockholm Skavsta (with Ryanair). The main hubs for connection flights from other Scandinavian airports to Dublin are London, Amsterdam and Copenhagen. Both carriers, Ryanair and SAS, may add additional direct flights during the summer months. www.flysas.com. www.ryanair.com

Flights To Dublin From Slovenia: Adria Airways offers direct flights from Ljubljana to Dublin in the summer months only. www.adria.si

Flights To Dublin From Switzerland: Direct flights to Dublin are available from Zurich and Geneva. Zurich is serviced by both Aer

Lingus and Swissair. The Geneva route is operated by Aer Lingus. www.swiss.com. www.aerlingus.com

Facts

Welcome to Dublin, the capital of Ireland. Famous for its easy going charm and cultural heritage, Dublin is also the capital of The Craic (pronounce 'crack'), the art of life. Famous Dublin sons such as writers Oscar Wilde, James Joyce and Jonathan Swift had it, playwright Samuel Beckett had it, and so have more contemporary cultural ambassadors such as U2. The city is steeped in rich history, starting with the Vikings laying its first streets. Through the centuries, The Craic and an unruly artistic streak have helped shape Dublin into what it is now: A vibrant capital that moves at an easy going pace.

Dublin's Location: Dublin is located on the East Coast of Ireland, stretching along the Irish Sea in a half moon shape. The city is bordered to the South by the dramatic Wicklow Mountains.

History of Dublin: From the invasion of the Vikings in the 8th Century through 700 years of Norman occupation, English rule and the formation of the Republic of Ireland in the 1920's, the city of Dublin has had a rich and varied history. Evidence of this can be found in every corner of the city. From a cultural point of view, that means plenty for visitors to see, from historic sites and landmarks to famous monuments and thought-provoking museums.

Foreign Embassies In Dublin: As the capital of Ireland, Dublin has a large number of foreign embassies offering a wide range of services to travellers. At the latest count, Dublin had a total of 53 embassies. Here you will find a list of all countries which maintain an embassy in Dublin as well as the embassies' address details and phone numbers.

Meet The Natives: The Dubliners: As a city, Dublin's character is firmly shaped by its people. Dubliners are a friendly and mildly inquisitive lot. Rarely will you venture into a pub without somebody standing near you striking up a conversation. If you ever find yourself lost, ask somebody and more than likely you'll be greeted with a little friendly chat. Dubliners are also known for their sharp wit and deadpan humour. Any bookshop in Ireland will sell you books of 'Dublin Humour'.

With three of Ireland's largest universities in town, Dublin is a very young city. Part of Dublin's charm is that all ages and all walks of life mix together. Particularly at night time, this mix makes for a lively and welcoming atmosphere in Dublin's myriad pubs, bars, restaurants, clubs and concert venues.

The Language: The language spoken in Dublin is English. Street signs and official buildings are signposted in both English and Gaelic, the indigenous Irish language. Despite this, you are highly unlikely to hear any Gaelic spoken on your travels across town. You are, however, likely to come across a lot of cursing in casual conversations. IRelax, it does not carry the same connotations it might in other languages.

The Currency: The currency in use in Ireland is the Euro. Cash machines (ATMs) are widely available. Bank opening hours are typically between 10:00-16:00 Mondays to Fridays. Most hotels, shops, restaurants and some bars accept all major credit cards. Visa and Master Card are the most widely used credit cards in Ireland. If you plan on visiting a pub it is advisable to bring some cash. You will also need cash for taxis and most public transport.

Opening Hours: Shops are typically open from 9:00-18:00 Mondays to Saturdays. Many shops are open late on Thursdays and Fridays (typically up to 20:00) and a good number is also open from 12:00-18:00 on Sundays. Pubs open at 10:30 and close at 23:30 Mondays to Thursdays, 0:30 on Fridays and Saturdays. On Sundays, pubs open 12:30 and close at 23:30. Clubs and late night bars typically stay open until 2:30.

Dublin's Two Halfs: North- And Southside: Dublin is a city of two halfs, the Northside and the Southside, divided by the River Liffey in the city centre. The Northside is generally more working class, the Southside is more upmarket. Exceptions apply, but by and large this is a good rule of thumb to apply when exploring the city. Dubliners on both sides can get very passionate about this division and it is the basis of many a joke or smart remark you may overhear in conversation.

<u>The Northside</u>: The Northside of the city is home to the main thoroughfare of Dublin, O'Connell Street, running north-south from Parnell Square, the city's most expensive address in the late 17th century, all the way to the Liffey. The central location of the 1916 Rising, the General Post Office (GPO to Dubliners), is located halfway down O'Connell Street. Henry Street off O'Connell Street is a popular <u>shopping district</u>. Only in Dublin could you find a traditional vegetable market in the middle of it all: Turn off Henry Street into Moore Street and mix with the hustle and bustle of a working street market.

The Northside is also home to many museums, theatres, Croke Park Stadium and to Phoenix Park, Europe's largest city park which houses <u>Dublin Zoo</u>.

<u>The Southside</u>: On the Southside, you find the bohemian <u>Temple Bar</u> district with its galleries and <u>nightlife</u>, the main <u>shopping area</u> centred around Grafton Street and the delightful park Saint Stephens Green. In general, you find more trendy and unusual shops in the backstreets to the West of Grafton Street, particularly on Clarendon Street, William Street South, Drury Street and Wicklow Street and Exchequer Street to the North.

The Southside is also home to Ireland's oldest and most famous university, Trinity College, the Government Buildings, <u>Dublin Castle</u>, Lansdowne Road Stadium and the oldest parts of the city around Christchurch Cathedral and St Patrick's Cathedral.

The Outskirts: Venture South along Dublin Bay and you will come to some of Dublin's most picturesque spots. The scenery changes rapidly from flat sandy beaches to rocky cliffs and coves harbouring picture perfect seaside towns and harbours. Sandycove, Dalkey and Killiney have presevered an old world charm. On a sunny day, you can even find an almost Mediterranean atmosphere here. To the North of Dublin you find Howth, a major fishing harbour and Malahide, a quaint seaside town with a park and romantic 19th century castle.

Area Guide

Dublin has a very compact centre while the majority of the city has preserved a distinctive village feel that is unusual for a European city its size. Take a 10 minute bus ride from O'Connell Street or College Green and you find yourself travelling through a patchwork quilt of villages and towns, each with their own individual character. From posh, rugby playing Ballsbridge to the echoes of former Victorian glory in the seaside resort of Bray, Dublin offers a fascinating mix of local styles and atmospheres.

Dublin City Centre

The centre of Dublin has a very organic feel to it, with its winding, narrow streets and low buildings. There is only one grand avenue in the centre and that is O'Connell Street. The rest of the streets is much more human in scale. Few buildings in the city centre are more than four stories high and an appealing mix of 18th century Georgian and 19th century Victorian styles dominates most streets in the centre. Life in Dublin's city centre is charming, slightly chaotic and fairly laid back.

Dublin's Hub: Dublin has a hub and spokes structure, with the centre as the hub and outlying areas as the spokes. Because of the relatively small size of Dublin, most fresh impulses and ideas start in the centre to reach the biggest possible audience. New shops, bars and nightclubs invariably operate from a city centre location and there are still enough up and coming areas waiting to be discovered, which keeps rents low for innovative start-ups. Because all the new places are in the centre, everybody comes here from the 'burbs and the cycle repeats itself.

The People: Another sign of the centre's role as the hub is the mix of people, which is much more diverse and colourful in the centre than in most of the suburbs and surrounding areas. Afro-Caribbean shopkeepers mingle with ancient Dublin market traders on Moore Street while art students with retro 1980's hairdos rub shoulders with conservative South County Dublin shoppers on College Green, barely a five minute walk away. With just over a million people living in the greater Dublin area, the city centre is the most convenient meeting place for everybody.

City Centre Sights: Sights located within Dublin's city centre include Trinity College, Dublin Castle, Dublinia, the Hugh Lane Gallery, the National Museum Of Ireland - Archaeology, the Science Gallery as well as the city's two most picturesque parks, St. Stephen's Green and Merrion Square, the main shopping mile Grafton Street and the cultural and nightlife hot spot Temple Bar. Dublin's most famous churches, St. Patrick's Cathedral and Christchurch Cathedral, are both located within a five minutes' walk of each other in the city centre. You could easily visit all the main sites in the city centre within a day without breaking into a sweat.

Old Dublin: If you want to see some of the oldest parts of Dublin, hop on a 123 Bus anywhere on Dame Street between Trinity and Dublin Castle and get off at Thomas Street. This area to the West of St. Patrick's Cathedral and up to Meath Street and Thomas Street is the ancient heart of the city. The area is pretty run down and neglected, but the warren of streets and the tiny cottages give you a good idea of the cramped living conditions that drove Dubliners out to the comparatively clean and positively spacious suburbs in the 19th century. There are pockets of new life in the ancient city centre, particularly on Francis Street with its art galleries and the Tivoli theatre. The Vicar Street music venue is loacated at the top of Thomas Street and there are new bars and shops opening up in what is still a predominantly poor area. Check out the shops and indoor market on

Meath Street for a glimpse into Dublin inner city life away from the bright lights of Grafton Street.

New Dublin: The newest parts of the city centre are located East of Trinity College's campus, around Grand Canal Dock on the South Bank of the River Liffey and on North Wall Quay on the Liffey's North Bank. Once a deserted labyrinth of warehouses, the area will house Dublin's new conference centre, a major new theatre and some of the city's most striking high rise buildings. There is still a lot of construction work going on, but restaurants and bars have already made inroads into the area, particularly around Grand Canal Dock.

Getting Around Dublin City Centre: The 123 bus is one of the most useful routes in the city centre. It connects O'Connell Street with Thomas Street and beyond, taking in Trinity, Grafton Street, Temple Bar and Dublin Castle inbetween. If you want to venture down Wexford Street and Camden Street for some nightlife or restaurants, you can hop on a 16 or 16A bus anywhere between O'Connell Street and Dame Street. The Red Luas is handy for exploring the Northside from East to West, from the shopping on Henry Street to the pubs around Smithfields and the Four Courts. The Green Luas on the Southside leaves the city centre too soon to be of much use.

Bray Dublin

Located 20 kilometres South of Dublin, Bray is the largest town in Ireland with a population of 36,000. While some of its outskirts are located in County Dublin, the centre of Bray lies in County Wicklow. Bray is a seaside town with an air of faded glamour dating back to its Victorian heyday. A bit tattered around the edges, Bray is still worth a daytrip from Dublin on the Dart local railway. Some of the most scenic walks around Dublin lead from Bray Head over steep cliffs to the neighbouring town of Greystones, offering magnificent sea views.

History Of Bray: From Norman times until the 17th century, Bray was a small fishing harbour on the borders of the Anglo-Irish heartland, The Pale, from which the English colonialised Ireland. When the coastal railway from Dublin reached Bray in 1854, the town reinvented itself as a seaside resort and became an overnight success. Bray remained a popular beach holiday destination with Irish and UK holidaymakers until the 1970's and the advent of cheap international travel. The town has yet to recover from the loss of the tourist business. Bray today is basically a commuter town, offering affordable housing to workers with jobs in Dublin.

Bray Today: Bray is full of faded glamour from its days as a popular seaside resort. The 1.5 kilometre long promenade with its bandstand and pavilions is still there and so are the former Victorian hotel buildings with their large panoramic dining room windows overlooking the beach. Unlike Brighton in the UK, Bray has not yet discovered the bohemian vibe that goes so well with faded seaside towns. Once you leave the beach and walk land inwards you will discover a pretty dreary shopping town that services rural Wicklow, crowded with the usual chain stores and fast food outlets.

Bray Head: It may only rise 241 metres over sea level, but Bray Head nevertheless offers dramatic cliff views over the Irish Sea. The unspoiled countryside has been protected since 2008 and offers the best hill walking in the Dublin area. On top of Bray Head you can see a concrete cross which was erected in 1950. Once a year on Good Friday, a procession makes its way up Bray Head from the town to mark the stations of the Cross. The final station is held at the cross on the hill top.

Ardmore Studios: Ireland's only purpose built film studios are located in Bray. The Ardmore Studios were opened in 1958 on instigation of the Irish government and attract international and Irish filmmakers. More than 100 movies were made at Ardmore in the last 50 years. Some of the movie classics shot at Ardmore include The Spy Who Came In From The Cold (1965), My Left Foot (1989), The Commitments (1991), In the Name Of The Father (1993), Braveheart (1995), The Tailor Of Panama (2001) and Breakfast On Pluto (2005). Ardmore is also popular with TV producers and recent TV work includes the successful historical soap opera The Tudors. www.ardmore.ie

Entertainment: You can get a good pint of Guinness and plenty of atmosphere in Harbour Bar on Dargle Road, close to the Dart station. Probably due to the vicinity of Ardmore Studios, the Harbour Bar is often turned into a film set. Don't let that put you off, the Harbour Bar has character, which is sadly missing from many other places in town which succumbed to half-hearted attempts at modernisation. There are plenty of restaurants and fast food joints in Bray. For the real seaside experience, have some fish and chips at Cassoni's on Strand Road.

How to Get to Bray: Bray's success as a commuter town has a lot to do with the reliable and convenient Dart local railway service that connects the town with Dublin's city centre. Bray station is located close to the seafront and deposits you straight at the heart of the action if you come as a day-tripper.

Ballsbridge Dublin

Ballsbridge is arguably Dublin's most exclusive address. Streets such as Shrewsbury Road and Ailesbury Road boast the highest real estate prices in Ireland with asking prices of up to €50 million for a single property. The area has traditionally been the home of the majority of foreign embassies and diplomatic representations in Dublin. It is not hard to see why the rich and powerful come to Ballsbridge: Originally developed in Victorian times, the streets are wide and tree lined and houses are substantial and set back in vast private grounds. Of all

Dublin areas, Ballsbridge has the least built-up and most 'private' feel. Yet, despite the space and relative tranquility, Ballsbridge is only minutes away from the city centre.

Ballsbridge History: The area is named after Balls Bridge, a three-arched cut stone bridge built over the River Dodder in 1791. Development began some fifty years later, when the Earl of Pembroke leased out his vast estates in the area and large red brick houses were built for upper class families. City politics at the time gave Ballsbridge its exclusive air: Planning regulations at the time decreed that houses for the working class were restricted to Irishtown and Ringsend to the North East of Ballsbridge.

The RDS: The Royal Dublin Society (RDS) was founded in 1731 with the aim to promote and develop Irish agriculture, arts, industry and science. Originally located in the city centre, the RDS moved to the newly developed Ballsbridge leasing 15 acres of land in 1879. The first shows took place in Ballsbridge in 1881. In 1926 the RDS held the first Aga Khan Trophy contest during its annual Horse Show. The Agha Khan Trophy has since grown to become the World's most prestigious contest for show jumping. In recent years, the RDS has widened its programme to house all sorts of events at its Ballsbridge grounds. Arts shows, musicals, rock concerts, fun fairs and ice skating rinks are just part of what the RDS offers. www.rds.ie

Rugby: Ballsbridge is steeped in rugby. Nowhere else in Dublin will you find a similar concentration of rugby clubs and playing fields. Rugby originated in the 1820's at English universities. The oldest rugby club in Ireland is Dublin University, which dates back to 1854. Given Ballsbridge's nature as an almost exclusively upper class enclave in Victorian times, it is no wonder that the second rugby club would spring up here: The Wanderers were founded in 1870 by an ex-Dublin University player. Today, Ballsbridge and neighbouring Donnybrook are home to half a dozen active rugby clubs. Apart from the Wanderers you find Old Belvedere, Lansdowne, Old Wesley, Leinster Rugby Club and the Bective Rangers all practically within spitting distance from each other. www.dufc.ie. www.oldbelvedere.ie. www.wanderersfcrugby.com

Lansdowne Road Stadium: Given Ballsbridge's taste for rugby, it is no surprise that one of the oldest international stadiums in the world is located here. The first international rugby match was held at Lansdowne Road Stadium as early as 1878. The first stand was added in 1908 and the stadium has been the home of Irish rugby until it closed down for a total rebuilt in 2007. The old Lansdowne Road stadium has been completely razed, giving way to a new, state-of-the-art 50,000 seater stadium. The new stadium is due to open at Lansdowne Road in early 2010. Following a ten year sponsorship deal with Ireland's largest insurance company, Hibernian Aviva, the Lansdowne Road site will now be called the Aviva Stadium.

Herbert Park: Herbert Park is a green oasis spread over 32 acres of prime Ballsbridge land. It is named after Sidney Herbert, the father of the Earl of Pembroke who owned the land that Ballsbridge was built on. Some features of the park date back to the Dublin International Trades Exhibition, a kind of mini World Fair held in Dublin in 1907. Herbert Park these days offers football pitches, tennis courts, boules, croquet lawns and a children's play ground to the public.

Eating Out in Ballsbridge: Eateries and pubs in Ballsbridge concentrate around Ballsbridge village, which is located on Pembroke Road and Merrion Road, just before you get to the RDS. Pubs here include Paddy Cullen's, Crowe's, Mary Mac's and Bellamy's, all of which serve pub food throughout the day. Popular restaurants in Ballsbridge are Roly's Bistro, The Lobster Pot and the picturesque Bella Cuba. With so much multi-million Euro real estate close by, restaurants are relatively pricey and the cooking is on the staid, conservative side. The pubs around Ballsbridge are largely dominated by sports fans who are predominantly into rugby. Try the bar and restaurant at stylish new boutique hotel The Dylan for something a little different.

Foreign Embassies: More than half of the foreign embassies in Dublin are located in Ballsbridge. Some 29 out of 53 embassies are spread across Ballsbridge's leafy streets, including the American Embassy in Dublin, the British Embassy, the Embassy of France, the Embassy of

Italy, the Embassy of Spain, the Polish Embassy and the Embassy Of The Netherlands.

Getting to Ballsbridge: Ballsbridge can be conveniently reached by DART local railway services. The main DART stops are Lansdowne Road for the Northern parts of Ballsbridge and Sandymount for Southern parts including the RDS. The Sydney Parade station services the Southernmost tip of Ballsbridge at the top of Aylesbury Road. Bus routes 4, 5, 7, 7A, 7E, 8, 18, 45, 63 and 84 all go through Ballsbridge.

Dublin Area History:

The strong sense of individuality among Dublin's areas dates back centuries, when many of these former villages and towns competed with Dublin on economic grounds. Rathmines, only 10 minutes South from St. Stephen's Green, was a wealthy town in the 19th century. You can still see the imposing bourgeois glamour of the former town's triumvirate of city hall, church and fire station. Further South in County Dublin, Dalkey was Dublin's principal port throughout the middle ages and Dun Laoghaire started as a major Victorian seaside resort that Dubliners would visit for a day trip by train. Malahide to the North of the centre prospered thanks to Malahide Castle and its associated farmlands as well as an important harbour.

Rathmines Dublin

imilar to Ballsbridge, Rathmines started as an elegant residential town for wealthy Dubliners who fled the cramped streets of the city centre in the mid-19th century. Unlike Ballsbridge, the dream did not last. The once grand townhouses had fallen into a sad state of repair and were split into hundreds of tiny flats in the 1960s and 70s, earning Rathmines the nickname 'Flatland'. The cheap flats brought students and immigrants from all corners of the world and the new, slightly bohemian atmosphere is beginning to attract new interest in the area. Situated just South of the Grand Canal and rubbing shoulders with posher Donnybrook to the East, Rathmines with its predominantly Victorian red brick housing stock full of character is worth a short detour.

Rathmines History: Before the bourgeois exodus from Dublin in the 19th century, Rathmines was a sparsely inhabited, rural hinterland, part of the Barony of Uppercross to the South of Dublin. Oliver Cromwell's troops came here to fight it out with the Royalist forces in Ireland at the Battle of Rathmines on the 2nd of August 1649. Some 5,000 men died that day and the battle effectively put Cromwell in charge of Ireland. Ratmines heyday began in 1847, when it became a town by Act of Parliament. Rathmines prospered and in its glory days acquired a copper dome originally destined for St Petersburg to crown its flagship church, Mary Immaculate, Refuge of Sinners in 1922. The township did not even last 100 years and Rathmines was integrated into the City of Dublin in 1930. The descent into 'Flatland' followed suit and despite pockets of gentrification, Rathmines is still a bit grubby around the edges.

Rathmines Today: Small shops and fast food outlets dominate Rathmines' main thoroughfares. You get the usual range of chain stores, but also a number of unique, one-off shops you won't find anywhere else. From old fashioned delicatessen like Fothergills and Lawlors to Asian and Middle Eastern stores and chic modern shops like Field & Vine, Rathmines has preserved a bit of character. For a glimpse of Rathmines' former glory, visit the Mary Immaculate church and the Rathmines Library on the main drag, Lower Rathmines Road.

Rathmines Nightlife: Chinese, Japanese, Thai and Indian restaurants vie for attention on Rathmines main street. There is also a trendy burger joint, Jo Burger, on Rathmines Road and the small, bistro-like Wild Lily. Rathmines has a good number of pubs which get particularly busy after office hours. Slattery's and Mother Reilly's are old fashioned Dublin pubs while Toast and the Madison Bar aim for a more urban, modern look.

How to Get to Rathmines: The Beechwood stop on the Green Luas line is the nearest stop for most amenities in Rathmines. Bus routes 14, 14A, 15, 15A and 83 connect Rathmines with the city centre.

County Dublin

County Dublin is much larger than the city of Dublin itself and stretches from the coastal town of Balbriggan in the North to Shankill in the South. Dublin is the third smallest County in Ireland and shares borders with Meath, Kildare and Wicklow. Even though half of the County's area is located to the North of the city, the term 'County Dublin' is most commonly used by Dubliners to describe the commuter towns and coastal villages on the Southside. A more precise term would be 'South County Dublin', but you will find both used to describe the lush, generally wealthy 'burbs in the South.

Dublin County Councils: County Dublin is split into four administrative councils, Dublin City council, Fingal to the North, the confusingly named South Dublin to the West and Dun Laoghaire Rathdown to the South. Fingal accounts for almost half of the County's 920 square kilometres but only 20% of the population. Nearly half of the County's population lives in Dublin City.

South County Dublin: County Dublin is home to many of Ireland's rich and famous. And even though Malahide in the North is every bit as expensive and exclusive as Dalkey in the South, it is South County Dublin with its string of picturesque coastal villages that is synonymous with the Dolce Vita in Ireland. Even without the flash cars and imposing gates you know you've come somewhere special. The landscape takes on a Mediterranean, somehow Italian atmosphere once you leave Dun Laoghaire and head South as Dublin Bay transforms from grey tidal mud flats to soaring cliffs and turquoise waters studded with palms and pine trees. Moving from Glasthule over Sandycove to Dalkey you will swear you've left Dublin and entered a different country.

The 40 Foot: Take the DART to Sandycove/Glasthule station and walk from Scotsman's Bay to Sandycove Harbour, continue up the hill and you will find the 40 Foot bathing place. Hardy Dubliners com here all year round to swim in the Irish sea. The concrete wind shelters of the 40 Foot are perched on an impressive rock outcrop reaching into the bay and concrete steps lead you right into the crashing waves of the Irish Sea. Swimmers would traditionally go in naked and the bathing place was open for men only. A lot has changed in the last ten years or so and swimming trunks or wetsuits are now the norm. Follow the road that curves away from the 40 Foot, continue up the hill and you will see a 19th century fortified tower on your right. It is one of a string of Martello Towers dotted along Dublin's coastline.

The Martello Tower: The string of Martello Towers stretches along most of County Dublin's shoreline, from Malahide in the North to Dalkey in the South. The towers were part of a coastal early warning and defence system around Dublin Bay that was supposed to deter Napoleon's fleet. The Martello Tower in Sandycove Harbour houses a fine little museum dedicated to Irish author James Joyce.

Vico Road : Drive up Vico Road in Dalkey for some of the most stunning views to be had in Dublin, from Dalkey Island over Killiney Bay to the Wicklow Mountains. For maximum effect, come here in a convertible or on a motorbike. If you are travelling by public transport, take the DART local railway service, get off at Killiney station and walk back up Vico Road towards Dalkey.

From Vico Road To Dalkey: At the end of Vico Road turn right into Sorrento Terrace and then left into Coliemore Road which follows the coast and brings you into the Dalkey village. Reward yourself with a pint in Dalkey village before hopping back on the DART into town. Please note that this walk will involve some steep climbs. Good walking shoes are recommended.

Fishing In County Dublin: Sea Angling is one of Dublin's democratic sports. All ages are into it, from kids to pensioners, and you meet people with all sorts of backgrounds at the popular fishing spots. Some of the most popular spots are spread over South County Dublin with its rocky shoreline and crystal clear waters. Good fishing spots are generally marked by the local council with brown and white sign posts. Just ask in a local shop or pub for the nearest fishing spot or follow the signs from the main road. Mackerel fishing in late summer is a typical Dublin pastime. You do not need a license for sea angling in Ireland and the only expense you will incur is for the rod, line and lure. Please note, that a license is required if you intend to fish for salmon or sea trout.

Boat Trips Along The County Dublin Coast: If you want to head out onto the water, have a look at South County Dublin's coast from the sea and maybe throw in a bit of sea angling, then head out to Bullock Harbour. The tiny fishing harbour is located halfway between Dalkey and Glasthule. You can walk here from either DART station. Car parking is available but fairly limited. During the Summer there are usually boats for hire here, weather permitting.

Boat hire will cost €20-€30 per hour. For more information, call +353 (0)1 280 6517 or 280 0915 for boat rental in Bullock Harbour. Please note, boats are very popular, so it is advisable to call early.

There is another small harbour in Dalkey, Coliemore Harbour. Tiny as it looks today, it used to be Dublin's main port in the Middle Ages thanks to Dalkey charging lower duties than Dublin City. Phone +353 (0)1 283 4298 for information on boat hire at Coliemore Harbour.

Getting Around County Dublin: The DART local railway service is the most convenient way to travel in South County Dublin. The DART stops at all coastal villages between Dun Laoghaire and Bray. The journey from Dalkey to Bray is particularly impressive as the DART tracks have been carved out from the cliff face towering over the Irish Sea. Bus routes 59 and 59A connect Glasthule, Sandycove, Dalkey and Killiney with the city centre.

Malahide Dublin

Malahide is a seaside town that grew around a Norman castle some 16 kilometres North of Dublin city centre. Cotton mills, salt works and a sizeable harbour made Malahide prosperous. Today, its secluded plots, large houses and splendid sea views make Malahide a favourite with well-to-do Dubliners looking for an alternative to Dalkey or Killiney in South County Dublin. Malahide is also very convenient for Dublin airport, which increases its attraction on the Irish jet set considerably. It is an easy day trip out from Dublin's city centre and you can while away the day on the grounds of Malahide Castle and a promenade along the seafront.

Malahide History: The Vikings came first and used to anchor their long ships in the sheltered estuary in between raiding expeditions along the Irish coast. The Normans came next and staid for good. The name Malahide or Mullach Íde in Irish is thought to date back to the 12th century and can be translated as 'Sandhills of the Hydes', a Norman family from the area. The ruling Norman family in Malahide where the Talbots and Sir Richard Talbot became the first Lord of Malahide around 1180. The Talbots built Malahide Castle which still stands today, if much refurbished over the centuries. Malahide was a thriving industrial town by the 18th century with silk and cotton mills and important salt works extracting the white gold from the Irish Sea. The railway arrived in the mid-1800s and brought wealthy Dubliners looking for more spacious living quarters.

Malahide today: In the last ten years, Malahide has become the des-res address in North County Dublin. Pop star Ronan Keating and chick lit author Cecelia Ahern live in Malahide. Actor Stephen Rea, U2 drummer Larry Mullen and U2 guitarist The Edge own properties in the Marina Village. Malahide is a pleasant little town and you can reach Malahide Castle and a selection of pubs and cafes within easy walking distance from the train station. A 20 minutes' walk along the coast towards Portmarnock brings you to some nice sandy beaches.

Malahide Castle: Malahide Castle was founded by Sir Richard Talbot, Lord of Malahide, in 1185. The Talbot family lived here until the last heir of the dynasty, Milo Talbot, died in 1973. The castle and its grounds were sold to the County Council in 1975 to cover the Talbot family's debts. The grounds stretch over a massive 109 hectares and include an 18th-century landscaped park as well as a cricket pitch, football pitches, a nine-hole par-three golf course and several tennis courts. Malahide Castle is open all year round and admission is free. The castle grounds regularly host open air concerts and festivals during the summer. Recent events at Malahide Castle included live gigs by Radiohead and Neil Young and the Lovebox dance music and indie festival

Malahide Marina: Malahide Marina has 350 fully serviced berths and can accommodate vessels up to 75 metres and 4 metres draught alongside. There is good room to manoeuvre in and out of the Marina and the Malahide Estuary is pretty sheltered. The Marina charges a flat rate of €12.00 per boat for short stays up to five hours. Regular daily rates start from €3.90 per metre and monthly berth rates from €61.00 per metre, excluding electricity and waste. There is a restaurant and a ship's chandlers shop on the premises. Other facilities include a moveable barbecue dock, satellite TV and 24-hour security. www.malahidemarina.net

Malahide Golf Club: One of the oldest golf clubs in Ireland, Malahide Golf Club was founded in 1892. The 27-hole, Par 71 course is located between Malahide and Portmarnock and was originally designed in a parkland style by Eddie Hackett. In 2007 the Blue Nine was redeveloped by Jeff Howes. Green fees on weekdays start from as little as 20.00 if you go with a member or 60.00 for guests. www.malahidegolfclub.ie

How to Get to Malahide: Malahide lies on the main Dublin-Belfast railway line and many commuter trains to Dundalk or Belfast stop here. The station is also served by the DART local railway. Bus route 42 connects Malahide with Dublin's city centre.

City Expansion

As Dublin grew as a city, new roads and buildings just filled the gaps between the different villages and towns. The main expansion phases of the city took place in the 1920's, the 1950's and the 1990's. Most

Dubliners live in one-storey terraced or semi-detached houses, which mix easily with the town centres that were there long before the city arrived on their doorsteps. High rise buildings are only a very recent addition that came with the explosion in Dublin land prices during the real estate boom of the late 1990s. So far, high rises are mainly limited to the city centre and a few new satellite towns like Sandyford and Blanchardstown.

Shopping And Restaurants: Dublin's outer areas are fascinating not only for their architectural merit or history but because they are thriving communities with often unusual shops and good restaurants. Many a fashion trend or celebrated chef started here before moving to the city centre. Check out the Blackrock Market, a covered flea market in Blackrock village, for a taste of what fashions might hit the small boutiques off Grafton Street next. Or sample classic Irish seafood at the celebrated Caviston's delicatessen and restaurant in Glasthule, County Dublin. Some shops are quaintly old-fashioned and survive because Dubliners will travel miles to get to a particular place that has a good reputation.

Dublin Area Events: In recent years, some of Dublin's suburbs have launched regular local events that vie for attention with those in the city centre during the summer. Blackrock organises summer festivals in a park on the seafront, Rathmines has its music and arts festival and Dun Laoghaire hosts an annual festival of World culture which features artists from Africa, Asia and Latin America. <u>Ballsbridge</u> is home to the Royal Dublin Society showgrounds, the largest event space in the Dublin. You will find a wide range of events here from show jumping for horses to rock concerts and art fairs.

Getting Around The Dublin Area: The DART local railway connects the city centre with all major areas that border on the coastline, from <u>Malahide</u> in the North over <u>Blackrock</u> and <u>Bray</u> to Greystones in <u>County Wicklow</u>. You can catch the DART in the city centre from Connolly, Tara Street or Pearse Street stations. Once you move away from the coast, locals rely heavily on their cars to get around. <u>Stillorgan</u> and <u>Rathmines</u> are well connected to the city centre by bus. Other areas are less convenient to reach since most bus routes run North to South, connecting the centre with a particular suburb and there are few bus routes running between local areas.

Both <u>Tallaght</u> and <u>Sandyford</u> have a good Luas tram connection. Tallaght is at the end of the Red Luas line from Connolly. Sandyford has the Green Luas tram line which connects it with St. Stephen's Green in the city centre. But Sandyford's office and retail park is growing faster than the Luas tracks, so you may face a good walk from the Luas terminus to your destination.

Dublin By Area

Ballsbridge: Ballsbridge has been the urban retreat of choice for Dublin's wealthy citizens since the 19th century. With its posh airs and exclusive residences, Ballsbridge is the home to foreign embassies, several rugby clubs and the Royal Dublin Society with its annual horse show.

Blackrock: Georgian houses, art galleries and a 19th century park by the sea give the coastal suburb of Blackrock a bohemian feel. A swift Dart train connection with the city centre makes Blackrock a popular residential area with families looking for some fresh sea air.

Blanchardstown: Dublin's fastest growing suburb combines Dublin's biggest shopping centre with an old country town nestling on the North bank of the Royal Canal. In the spirit of contemporary urban living, the Blanchardstown Centre mall combines commerce and public amenities doubling up as the town centre.

Bray: A Victorian seaside town with a long pebble beach, Bray is a firm favourite with day-trippers from Dublin. The headland at the Southern end of town, Bray Head, offers spectacular views and good walks along the coast.

City Centre: For a city of a million inhabitants, Dublin has a very intimate and compact city centre. Narrow lanes, pedestrian zones and covered markets invite you to take a stroll and go exploring.

County Dublin: A string of pretty coastal towns and fishing harbours stretches from Dublin to the South. If you travel the coast from North to South the scenery changes from wind-blown sandy beaches to ragged cliffs and sheltered coves inviting you for a boat trip or a swim.

Malahide: The picturesque coastal town of Malahide lies a short train trip to the North of Dublin. A quaint town centre, 12th century Malahide Castle and a large marina make Malahide a great destination for a day trip from Dublin.

Rathmines: Bohemian, cosmopolitan Rathmines lies just South of the Grand Canal. Minutes away from the city centre, Rathmines has an easygoing pace of life and the atmosphere of a town within the city.

Sandyford: Once an office park by the side of the motorway, Sandyford now has a Luas tram connection into the city centre, the Beacon shopping centre and Dublin's first museum for children.

Stillorgan: A quiet suburb on Dublin's Southside, Stillorgan can boast to have Ireland's oldest shopping centre and offers a convenient location for nearby University College Dublin.

Tallaght: The sprawling commuter town of Tallaght is reinventing itself as a centre for the arts in the South West of Dublin. With the Luas tram line connecting Tallaght to the city centre, a flurry of building activity is giving the town a much needed facelift.

Wicklow: Wicklow, the county bordering on Dublin in the South, offers mountains, forests and kilometres of sandy beaches. If you would like to escape the city for a day, then Wicklow offers a number of destinations that can be easily reached from Dublin

The End